Acknowledgments

Many people provided invaluable help in the preparation of this paper. A large number of the papers used as references were obtained from the Human Interactions with Tropical Ecosystems project at the East-West Environment and Policy Institute (EAPI) in Hawaii. We are deeply indebted to Terry Rambo, director of the project, for the use of these files and to his colleagues—including Chris Gibbs, Gerry Marten, and Napoleon Vergara—for sharing their thoughts and written materials. Thanks also to Steve Gliessman, Miguel Altieri, Steve Risch, and Ron Carroll for their help during a similar reference-hunting trip in California. Bob Winterbottom, Mike McGuahey, and John Michael Kramer provided valuable references on agroforestry. Several reviewers provided detailed, extremely useful comments on earlier drafts of this study. Mohamed El-Ashry, Monty Yudelman, Bill Burley, and Jessica Mathews reviewed the first draft at WRI. Review comments from Gordon Conway, Gordon Harrison, Gary Toenniessen, Chris Hennin, Lester Brown, Tom Niblock, Peter Freeman, Ted Wolf, and Tom Edens on the second draft provided the basis for extensive revisions. Although we greatly appreciate the reviewers' time and attention, the study nonetheless remains our own, especially any errors that may have escaped our notice.

Most of all, we are indebted to the scores of field scientists who have worked over the years, often with little encouragement from the agricultural "establishment," to understand the ecological principles that form the basis for food production. Without them, alternative approaches to agriculture could not be the subject of a policy-oriented study such as this one.

M.J.D.
L.M.T.

TO FEED THE EARTH:
Agro-Ecology for
Sustainable Development

Michael J. Dover and Lee M. Talbot

D0471751

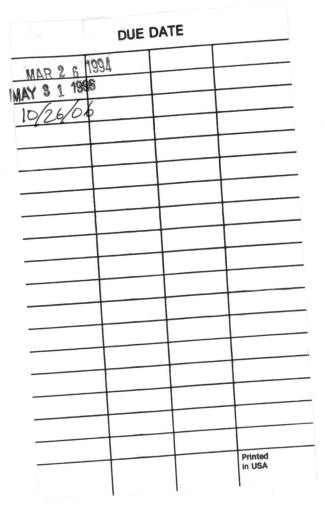
DUE DATE

MAR 2 6 1994

MAY 3 1 1996

10/26/06

Printed
in USA

WORLD RESOURCES INSTITUTE
A Center for Policy Research

June 1987

S
482
D68
1987

RASMUSON LIBRARY
UNIVERSITY OF ALASKA-FAIRBANKS

Kathleen Courrier
Publications Director

Myrene O'Connor
Marketing Manager

Hyacinth Billings
Production Supervisor

International Institute of Tropical Agriculture
Cover Photo

Each World Resources Institute Report represents a timely, scientific treatment of a subject of public concern. WRI takes responsibility for choosing the study topics and guaranteeing its authors and researchers freedom of inquiry. It also solicits and responds to the guidance of advisory panels and expert reviewers. Unless otherwise stated, however, all the interpretation and findings set forth in WRI publications are those of the authors.

Copyright © 1987 World Resources Institute. All rights reserved.
Library of Congress Catalog Card Number 87-50722
ISBN 0-915825-19-8
ISSN 0880-2582

Contents

Foreword

"To feed the earth" has a double meaning. In the 1970s, concern arose over a possible global food shortage. Experts debated whether the earth could ever produce enough food to feed all its people. Although the headlines have disappeared, the question remains valid, for after a decade of strong agricultural growth there were more hungry people in 1980—*before* the Sahelian drought—than there had been in 1970. Despite impressive increases in agricultural productivity, production growth in some areas was matched or outstripped by population growth, and in other cases international debt burdens and falling commodity prices combined to depress food imports to hungry countries.

Today's concerns are different. Although aggregate agricultural production, now and for the foreseeable future, is sufficient to feed everyone, not everyone can afford to buy food. So part of the problem is distribution or, alternatively, growing enough food where the hungry people are. Tied to this concern are questions about the sustainability of agricultural production systems, especially in developing countries. The soil that sustains crop plants needs to be "fed" as much as do the people who benefit from the food it produces. Worries about sustainability are not new, but are newly salient as growing numbers of people put increasing pressure on what are often marginal agricultural lands.

This paper defines and describes an ecological approach to agriculture that differs profoundly from the industrial approach that has dominated agricultural research and development for decades. Both have their place, but—as argued here—the main issue is how to incorporate the former into agricultural development.

In declaring the start of the "Decade of the Tropics,"* the International Union of Biological Sciences (IUBS) noted that knowledge of species structure and function and of interactions among species in groups, communities, and ecosystems is the foundation upon which rests "the rational management of natural and artificial ecosystems," notably agriculture. Yet, IUBS points out, "our knowledge of these

---

*"A Decade of the Tropics," Otto T. Solbrig and Frank B. Golley, *Biology International*, Special issue—February, 1983.

processes and relationships is almost entirely derived from temperate or polar species," and there is good reason to believe that tropical species and ecosystems are vastly different. The attempted transfer of agricultural systems based on temperate zone biology and developed country economics (that is, of systems requiring high levels of purchased inputs) to poor countries with unreliable transportation systems and tropical environments is often a fruitless effort to transplant a good system to an area where it simply won't work.

The idea is not to abandon the methods of industrial agriculture that have been so successful in the economic and ecological conditions for which they were designed, but to determine where such methods as mechanization, use of agricultural chemicals, and monoculture are and are not appropriate, and to develop alternative systems better suited to tropical climates and developing economies. This study lays out steps—stretching from basic research to the mechanics of international assistance—that must be taken if ecologically based agriculture is to contribute all it can to feeding the earth.

Jessica T. Mathews
Vice President and Research Director
World Resources Institute

I. Introduction

"Today," writes leading American agricultural administrator Sylvan Wittwer, "the world is awash in both grain and oil:"

Prices for each are expected to drop even lower than they are now. A decade ago both were considered in short supply and prices were going ever higher. Who, 10 years ago, would have predicted the present state of affairs?.... Near all-time food production records were achieved in 1984 by the United States, China, Indonesia, and many Western European countries. In Japan and Taiwan surplus rice is posing serious problems of land diversion to other crops. China and Indonesia are witnessing some of the most impressive gains in food production in history. For the first time in decades China is concerned with marketing, handling, and storing of food surpluses. Within four years Indonesia has moved from the world's largest importer of rice to a country not only self-sufficient but with the world's largest rice reserves.[1]

These words might lead one to question whether reviewing the problems of agriculture in developing countries is necessary. Yet, as Wittwer himself observes, rampant malnutrition, poverty, and starvation continue, and famine was more widespread in 1985 than in 1975. "This spectacle of world impotence toward too much food in some places and too little in others is especially shocking since it is man-made."[2]

While the United States and Western Europe struggle to deal with farm crises triggered by overproduction, many developing countries are hard-pressed to keep food production ahead of population growth. Indeed, the United Nations Food and Agriculture Organization (FAO) paints a rather dismal picture of Third World hunger in the next two decades if massive increases in agricultural production, coupled with stringent population control, are not achieved.[3] If agricultural technologies are applied as they are today, FAO projects, 64 countries—29 of them in Africa—will be unable to meet their populations' food needs by the turn of the century, even assuming that all cultivable land is under production. Even under its most optimistic scenario, FAO still expects at least 19 countries to fall below this critical mark by the year 2000.[4] *(See Table 1.)*

The inequities implicit in these projections are not simply at the global level. Despite increases in food production in many developing

Table 1. Number of Countries Considered "Critical"* by FAO						
				Region		
	Africa	S.W. Asia	S.E. Asia	South America	Central America	TOTAL
Total countries	51	16	16	13	21	117
Population (millions)						
1975	380	136	1118	216	106	1956
2000	780	265	1937	393	215	3589
No. of Critical countries:						
1975						
Inputs**						
Low	22	15	6	—	11	54
Interm.	7	12	1	—	4	24
High	2	9	1	—	1	13
2000						
Inputs						
Low	29	15	6	—	14	64
Interm.	12	15	2	—	7	36
High	4	12	1	—	2	19

*"Critical" means that the country cannot provide adequate nutrition to its population based on FAO/WHO recommended average calorie intake, assuming that *all* cultivable land is in production.

**Inputs refer to the level of agricultural technology applied; "low" indicates no agricultural chemicals or improved seeds and no long-term conservation measures; "intermediate" implies some chemicals and improved seeds, and conservation measures and improved cropping patterns used on half the land; "high" means full use of available technologies—equivalent to Western European levels of farming.

Source: Food and Agriculture Organization, *Land, Food and People* (Rome: Food and Agriculture Organization, 1984).

nations, the poor in these countries are not necessarily less poor or better fed. In some areas, their lot has worsened in part because new agricultural technologies make it more profitable for the rich to consolidate land holdings into large commercial farms, displacing tenant farmers and other smallholders in the process. If not exported, the food produced on these large farms may be sold not to the rural poor, but to the middle and upper classes who can afford it. For example, in the Philippines between 1975 and 1978, urbanites increased their calorie intake by over 10 percent, while their rural counterparts saw only a 2-percent rise. The poorest Filipinos in 1978 consumed fewer than 1,600 calories and about 43 grams of protein per day, compared to a nationwide average of 1,800 calories and 53 grams of protein, while the wealthiest group surveyed ate over 2,200 calories and nearly 73 grams of protein daily.[5] Figures like these suggest that even if food production outpaces population growth, there is no guarantee that malnutrition or starvation will subside.[6]

The world may indeed be awash in grain for the moment, but global demand for food continues to rise. Development planners are once again seeing agriculture as the mainstay of economic growth. And political and economic considerations are forcing many developing nations to seek self-sufficiency in food production. All of these factors place pressure on agricultural scientists and technologists to develop and teach methods to increase crop and animal production. To meet these goals, more land is being put under cultivation, use of existing land is being intensified, and high-yielding crop varieties and agricultural chemicals are being pressed on farmers. Whether any of these approaches will, in the long run, feed those most in need remains to be seen. Technology does not cause poverty or hunger, nor can technology alone end these ills. But rarely is the choice of which technologies to develop and use free of bias toward one social class or cultural group.[7] Perhaps as much as 80 percent of agricultural land today is farmed with little or no use of chemicals, machinery, or improved seed. As the world struggles to feed its ever-growing population, the appropriateness of new methods for peasant farmers may well be crucial.

Shrinking Resources, Future Priorities

Agriculture both causes and suffers from environmental degradation. Wittwer estimates that eight million hectares of land are lost annually to nonagricultural conversions, three million to erosion, and four million to desertification and toxification.[8] Pesticide and fertilizer pollution continue to provoke serious concern. Poisoning of farmworkers, contamination of food and water supplies, destruction of wildlife and fisheries, and pests' resistance to pesticides all contribute to a global awareness that agricultural chemicals can no longer be overused and misused.[9] Coupled with chemical dependence is a growing reliance on fossil fuels to run the world's major agricultural production systems. Can world agriculture afford to depend on a diminishing resource

The world may indeed be awash in grain for the moment, but global demand for food continues to rise.

Perhaps as much as 80 percent of agricultural land today is farmed with little or no use of chemicals, machinery, or improved seed.

3

that, despite current oversupply, is inherently limited? Can any nation's food security be assured if its soil fertility relies heavily on nitrogen fertilizer derived from fossil fuels? And can increasingly mechanized farms continue to function smoothly if fuel prices and supplies are unpredictable? These issues and others—such as deforestation, genetic erosion, and depletion of soil fertility—have prompted some in the international development community to address not only the productivity but the sustainability of agricultural systems.

Sustainability has come to mean different things to different people, but it most clearly has an ecological basis. Long before it was applied to agriculture, the concept of sustained yield was used in fisheries management to mean an annual harvest that could be taken in perpetuity—that is, from individuals in excess of those needed to maintain the population in roughly constant numbers. A similar idea can be applied to sustainable agriculture, though intensively managed systems and self-renewing natural systems differ in many ways. More generally, understanding the ecological basis of sustainability should lead to agricultural systems whose productivity can be continued indefinitely without undue degradation of other ecosystems.[10]

Considering sustainability in agriculture is essential because, regardless of short-term gains, *productivity without sustainability is mining.* Today, at the same time that energy conservation and other economizing measures are being introduced to conserve and recover such nonrenewable resources as fossil fuels and minerals, such so-called renewable resources as water, soil, and forests are being depleted at alarming rates. Record crops produced at the expense of the next year's or the next decade's soil resource are nothing to be proud of, whether in the United States or anywhere else. If agricultural and development institutions fail to address the sustainability of current or future farming practices, they will be doing a disservice to the very people they are trying to help.

Clearly, the productivity of the land must be improved. Even if the most conservative estimates of population growth prove true, fertile land is so limited that productivity of existing agricultural areas will have to increase to meet ever-growing needs. Both crop yields and cropping intensity must rise. *(See Table 2.)* But where? Certainly, current crop surpluses in the industrialized world can be used for emergency food aid if funds are available. However, because poor nations cannot pay for continuing food imports in the long run, production increases in North America or Europe can do little to prevent chronic malnutrition in Africa, Asia, and Latin America. Instead, productivity must be improved where the food is needed. Smallholders and tenant farmers must be able to feed their own families and generate modest surpluses, and commercial farms should be able to employ the landless, sell produce at affordable prices to those who need it, and turn reasonable profits. But these goals must be met without depleting soil, water, and the other natural resources on which continued agricultural productivity depends.

Productivity without sustainability is mining.

4

Table 2. Expected Contributions to Increases in Production in
90 Developing Countries, 1975–2000

| | Percent Contribution to Increase | | |
Region	Extension of cultivated areas of land	Farming intensity	Increased yield/ha.
Africa	27	22	51
Asia	10	14	76
Latin America	55	14	31
Middle East	6	25	69
All 90 nations	26	14	60

Source: FAO, *Agriculture: Toward 2000* (Rome: Food and Agriculture Organization, 1981).

Scientists and others concerned with agricultural development tend to see technology from one of two ends of a spectrum. At one extreme are those who maintain that the land's productivity can be increased only by introducing high-input and mechanized technologies based mainly on fossil-fuel energy, inorganic fertilizers, and chemical pesticides. At the opposite end from this "industrial" approach are advocates of an "ecological" approach—the development of more efficient low-input agricultural systems based on biological recycling of energy and chemical nutrients and reliance primarily on naturally occurring control mechanisms for crop protection.[11]

According to the U.S. Congressional Office of Technology Assessment, the industrial approach to agricultural development

> ...stresses production and increased yields. It tends to focus on a more limited number of crops for which a market already exists. The ecosystem is adjusted to provide high production of these crops by using intensive inputs of commercial fertilizers, pesticides, pumped water, and petroleum-powered farm equipment. Some such systems commonly are categorized as 'green revolution' technologies. Major efforts have been devoted to mainstay crops such as rice, corn, sorghum, and soybeans, and production increases generally have been outstanding.[12]

This industrial model is principally concerned with the flow of materials and money through the system. Its key measures are productivity (output per unit of land or labor) and economic efficiency (cash output per unit of cash input), and it requires considerable capital investment, infrastructure development, and extensive training of farmers.

The ecological approach considers cycles as well as flows in the system, and maintenance as well as productive functions. Its performance criteria are cycling rates, stability measures, and energy efficiency. This model of development seeks to apply

> ...biological technologies that are tailored to fit the biological, physical, and social limitations of the local environment so that sustainable agriculture can exist within the constraints of the natural resource base.... [It] also focuses on developing new agricultural systems and on accepting rediscovered, and perhaps improved, agricultural systems. A wide spectrum of agricultural crops is considered including a number that might be viewed as nontraditional. This approach emphasizes restoring, maintaining, and improving the natural resource base while offering farmers a reasonable chance for economic betterment.[13]

Obviously, the ecological paradigm—what agricultural publisher Robert Rodale calls regenerative agriculture[14]—depends upon a thorough understanding of the processes governing soil chemistry and biology, plant nutrition, and the forces that keep insects, pathogens, and weeds in check.

There is a place and a need for both approaches in world agriculture today, and much middle ground between them. Both can benefit from improved plant varieties, though each may select different characteristics and deploy improved strains differently. And both can effectively use methods of soil, water, and energy conservation, even though each approach will find different costs, risks, and benefits affecting the choice of specific techniques.

Advocating the wholesale abandonment of industrial agriculture would be inviting catastrophe. But that set of technologies has worked best under economic, social, and ecological conditions unlike those in large areas of the developing countries. (In Southeast Asia, for example, the "core areas" devoted to intensive Green Revolution food production account for less than 5 percent of the total land area.[15]) And often the productivity of the industrial approach has been achieved at the cost of an increasingly high energy subsidy and the depletion of soil, water, and other essential resources.

Few agriculturalists still want all vestiges of traditional farming practices replaced with "modern" methods. Many scientists and others now recognize the inherent practicality in much indigenous agriculture and the need to preserve both the knowledge and the valuable genetic materials embodied in these farming systems. But—under the pressure of increasing populations, migration, and cultivation of inappropriate lands—traditional agriculture is now a major contributor to environmental degradation in developing countries. And because yields in many traditional systems are low, pressure to clear new land for farming continues to increase.

As industrial methods have been imported and adapted to developing countries, food production has increased dramatically where conditions have been right. But attempts to transfer such technologies to farmers operating in less-than-ideal circumstances fail or even make things worse: yields drop after a short time, and soil erosion and other environmental degradation accelerates.

The growing need for a productive *and* sustainable agriculture calls for a new view of agricultural development that builds upon the risk-reducing, resource-conserving aspects of traditional farming, and draws on the advances of modern biology and technology. Key to this view—which is needed not only in the Third World but also to make farming in the industrialized countries more resource-efficient and environmentally sound—is a thorough understanding of agriculture's ecological underpinnings.

An Ecological Approach

Sustainability requires new directions for agricultural development, directions based on the principles and practical knowledge of ecology. Systems analysis—under such headings as integrated pest management and farming systems research—has proven of enormous help in organizing research and establishing project priorities. But, to be effective, a systems approach must be imbedded in a scientific discipline that addresses the appropriate level of organization to be studied and managed. In the case of agriculture, that level of organization is the agroecosystem and the appropriate discipline is ecology.[16]

All that ecologists study—the distribution, abundance, and inter-actions of organisms in space and time; the inter-relationships between organisms and the physical environment; and the flows of energy and materials through ecosystems—bears on our understanding of agroecosystems as whole systems and on the development of new technologies to support a sustainable agriculture. But two concepts—stability and diversity—are especially relevant. The several different meanings of ecosystem stability, their limits, and their apparent causes are especially important to understanding how to design and manage sustainable agricultural systems. The significance of species diversity in natural ecosystems bears close examination for its relevance to agriculture.

The application of some of these lines of thought to the study of agroecosystems has already begun.[17] Moreover, the intellectual and practical benefits obtained so far suggest that accelerating the process could pay off handsomely. For policy, the application of ecological principles to agriculture has potentially far-reaching implications. At the local or regional level, land tenure, farm size, and the structure of markets and services may need to be revamped.[18] National and international implementation of this approach could require changes in research and development priorities and greater interagency coordination than exists now. And on a global scale, an ecological view of agriculture could imply new concepts of economic development and development assistance.[19]

The challenge facing agriculture in the developing countries is daunting. Expanding populations must be fed—not just adequately, but well. Crushing debt loads and fuel import bills are creating enor-

The growing need for a productive and sustainable agriculture calls for a new view of agricultural development that builds upon the risk-reducing, resource-conserving aspects of traditional farming, and draws on the advances of modern biology and technology.

7

mous pressures to increase agricultural exports so as to obtain much-needed foreign exchange. And natural resources must be preserved as capital for future development and as the inheritance that future generations deserve. To meet these demands, agriculture must not only be more productive, but also economical and sustainable. The economics of agricultural development and equity among beneficiaries are beyond the scope of this paper. Yet, it must be emphasized that, no matter how economical a project may appear in the short term, its ecological viability will be a major factor in long-term success. We must feed the world today, but we must also feed the earth—its soil, water, plants, and animals—so that we can continue to feed the world tomorrow.

II. Environmental Constraints and Problems

Many environmental problems in developing countries stem from the misapplication of temperate-zone technologies to the tropics, where the ecological conditions facing agriculture differ markedly from those in temperate areas.[20] If productivity in these areas is to become sustainable, farming methods unique to the tropics will be needed to meet the unique constraints of temperature, rainfall, and soil conditions found there.

Tropical Environments

Climatologically, the tropics are diverse, encompassing deserts, semi-arid areas, and areas with the world's highest rainfall. If solar radiation and the growing season's length were the only considerations, the tropics might yield roughly twice as much per hectare per year as temperate areas. Rainfall, however, limits productivity in many parts of the tropics. Both excesses and deficits create problems, often in the same location. About half of the region has pronounced wet and dry seasons.[21] Much tropical rain falls in storms: 10 to 15 percent of rainy days with the heaviest storms contribute fully half of the annual rainfall, so most ecosystems cannot make full use of the water when it comes. And due to continually high temperatures, evaporation rates are high as well. The net result is high water deficits in many tropical agricultural areas: large cropland areas of Africa and India have water shortages comparable to temperate-zone deserts. Then too, rainfall varies tremendously in many tropical areas. In much of northern and sub-Saharan Africa, the Arabian Peninsula, and Western India, the year-to-year departure from average rainfall is over 40 percent, and in much of the rest of the tropics, the variation is over 20 percent.[22] Indeed, in parts of Africa, drought can cut yields in half if sowing is delayed as little as two weeks beyond the optimal planting date.[23]

The relatively high year-round temperatures of the tropics, the high incidence of solar radiation, and the small changes in daylength can also work against productive agriculture in the tropics. Since plants capture solar energy through photosynthesis, which is governed by the amount of solar radiation and the temperature, the tropics would

In parts of Africa, drought can cut yields in half if sowing is delayed as little as two weeks beyond the optimal planting date.

9

seem to have an advantage. But respiration—the consumption of the products of photosynthesis—also increases with temperature. In cereals, respiration occurs at about 35 percent of the photosynthetic rate in the tropics, compared to 25 percent in temperate climates. And the total amount of solar radiation available to crops in the tropics is substantially less than in temperate areas, both because tropical day-lengths are over two hours shorter than summer daylengths in the temperate areas, and because of widespread cloud cover during the tropics' rainy growing season. In semiarid and arid lands, long periods of sunlight are advantageous only in irrigated areas.[24]

These climatic conditions determine the structure and fertility of tropical soils. About 51 percent of these soils are highly weathered and leached—poor candidates for cropland kept fertile with conventional temperate-zone methods. *(See Table 3.)* With high rainfall causing leaching and high temperatures causing organic matter to

Table 3. Distribution of soils in the tropics (millions of hectares)

Soil type	Climatic region*				Percent of Tropics
	Rainy	Seasonal	Dry & Desert	Total	
Highly weathered, leached	920	1,540	51	2,511	51
Dry sands and shallow soils	80	272	482	834	17
Light-colored, base-rich	0	103	582	685	14
Alluvial	146	192	28	366	8
Dark-colored, base-rich	24	174	93	291	6
Moderately weathered and leached	5	122	70	207	4
Total area	1,175	2,403	1,316	4,896	100
Percent of tropics	24	49	27	100	

* Note: Rainy: 9.5–12 months with an average rainfall over 100 mm.
Seasonal: 4.5–9.5 months
Dry and Desert: 0–4.5 months

Source: P.A. Sanchez, *Properties and Management of Soils in the Tropics* (New York: John Wiley and Sons, 1976).

decompose rapidly, tropical forests have evolved into ecosystems that maintain most of their nutrients above ground in biomass. Up to 90 percent of the elements necessary for fertility may be tied up in trees, shrubs, and other plants in a tropical forest.[25] The soil itself in these incredibly lush habitats is virtually sterile. By comparison, in temperate-zone forests, as little as 3 percent of the nutrients are stored above ground. Cut a temperate-zone forest, and 97 percent of the nutrients available for new growth will remain in the soil. Cut a tropical forest, and almost all of these nutrients will be hauled away in the timber.[26]

Recent research suggests that the soil under tropical forests is not universally sterile, but that fertility can vary considerably from area to area. Still, the likelihood of soil sterility in some locations should make us think twice before clearing large forest tracts for farming.

Agricultural Adaptations and Consequences

Just as natural ecosystems have evolved to thrive under unique conditions, so too has traditional agriculture. Chief among the indigenous cropping systems have been the various techniques known as shifting agriculture, shifting cultivation, or swidden. This practice, common throughout the tropics, involves cutting and (usually) burning patches of forest to clear land for crops. Such fields are typically used for one to three years and then abandoned by farmers who move on to clear other plots. Burning releases the reservoir of nutrients in the plant material (though much of the nitrogen goes up in smoke), making the soil-ash mixture relatively fertile; it also kills most weeds. Once abandoned, plots are left fallow for several years. Exactly how long depends upon the availability of other land, the rate of regrowth of forest, and other factors. In general, the longer the fallow period, the more fertile the land will be when next cleared for crops. In Belize, Central America, for instance, even decade-long fallows could not restore lost phosphorus to the soil using traditional methods. Many farmers with plots idled for five to fifteen years reported crop failures, with plants showing symptoms of phosphorus deficiency.[27] In India, rice and maize yields on lands fallowed five to ten years were 98 percent and 48 percent lower, respectively, than yields in plots cleared after a 30-year fallow. At least ten years of fallow were needed to restore soil carbon, nitrogen, and humus after cropping.[28]

Swidden plots are not alone in suffering yield declines after a few growing seasons. In Thailand, repeated flooding and drying of paddy rice areas increases soil acidity over time, building up aluminum toxicity. In the Chiang Mai Valley, rice harvests averaged four tons per hectare in 1969 and rose to 6.4 tons by 1971 with fertilization and use of high-yielding varieties, but steadily declined to the 1969 levels by 1977. Perhaps more disturbing, yields became about twice as variable during that time.

When settled agriculture (such as paddy rice production) breaks down, when population pressure and land hunger cause farmers to shorten swidden fallow periods, when farmers apply lowland methods

Cut a temperate-zone forest, and 97 percent of the nutrients available for new growth will remain in the soil. Cut a tropical forest, and almost all of these nutrients will be hauled away in the timber.

Agriculture is both the cause and the victim of worldwide environmental degradation.

on upland soils, and when temperate-zone technologies are transferred wholesale to the tropics, the environmental consequences can be devastating. Agriculture is both the cause and the victim of worldwide environmental degradation. In the tropics, the very existence of the resource base that is the hope of development is threatened by deforestation, land degradation, pesticide problems, and impaired water-holding capacity of the land.

The United Nations Environment Programme (UNEP) estimates that 12 million hectares of tropical forests are lost annually.[29] Others put the figure as high as 21 million, of which about half is attributable to conversion to shifting agriculture.[30] Even if the conservative figure is correct, almost 1,400 hectares of tropical forest are lost each hour. According to UNEP, nine countries will have destroyed virtually all of their closed-forest cover by the year 2002, and another 13 countries will reach the same end 25 years later. (Together, these nations now contain 11 percent of the world's total closed forest.[31]) In Peninsular Malaysia, forests covered 74 percent of the country in 1957; twenty years later, those forests accounted for only 55 percent of the land. By 1980, about 285,000 hectares of forest land were being converted to agricultural use every year. Thirty-eight percent of the Philippines was forested in 1976, down from 75 percent at the end of World War II; the current rate of conversion to agricultural use has been estimated at 50,000 hectares per year.[32] On the Philippine island of Negros, the number of farmers practicing shifting cultivation increased by 80 percent in just two years; researchers predict that one major rain forest there will vanish by the turn of the century.[33]

If the population of shifting cultivators in tropical forests stays low, the practice poses relatively little threat to the survival of the forests. But for a variety of reasons—general population increases, displacement of tenant farmers from rented land, economic necessity—the number of farmers trying to eke out a living in this way has increased. With more farmers using the land, fallow periods have been shortened, and the spaces between plots reduced or eliminated. As a result, in many parts of the tropics, the forest cannot grow back. In some areas, forests have been replaced with permanent grassland, often dominated by one or two species of such grass as *Imperata cylindrica*. Indonesia has some 12 to 15 million hectares of such land, while the Philippines has about 5 million. According to Filipino ecologist Percy Sajise, the frequent fires that sweep these grasslands prevent regrowth of the forest and increase soil erosion. Moreover, soil fertility is reduced, productivity is marginal and unstable, and the hydrology of the area is disrupted, so both summer drought and rainy-season floods now occur more often.[34]

Loss of tropical rainforest has contributed to drought in Indonesia, reduction in the flow of water supplying the Panama Canal, "embryo deserts" in northern Brazil, clogging of Thailand's waterway transport system, and a drastic decline in the efficiency of hydroelectric dams in the Philippines.[35] Also in the Philippines, deforestation has been implicated in the eutrophication of lakes, which threatens local supplies of fish and drinking water.[36] Forest clearing also typically increases nutrient runoff, especially in hilly areas. Nutrient levels in runoff water at one site increased from two to eight times when trees were removed.[37] When these nutrients end up in lakes, they promote the growth of algae, often making the water unsuitable for fish.

Shifting cultivators are not solely responsible for tropical deforestation. The pressing need for firewood in many parts of the world is another major cause, as is increased commercial logging and the conversion of forest to commercial pasture to produce meat for export markets. Still, if half of the loss of rainforest is due to the expansion of agriculture, much can be gained by devising alternatives to the continued destruction that necessity forces these farmers to wreak. If agricultural technologies would allow them to farm without periodically clearing new sites, pressure on remaining forests could be reduced. And if those technologies can also help farmers produce more food on a sustainable basis, both people and land will benefit.

Deforestation is a major contributor to soil erosion. For instance, erosion rates increased from 200- to over 5,000-fold when African forest land was cleared. *(See Table 4.)* Sylvan Wittwer's estimate of five million hectares of cropland annually lost to erosion and desertification[38] appears conservative compared to UNEP's assertion that some six million hectares are being reduced to desert-like conditions every year, with an additional 14 million made entirely unproductive. Worldwide, says UNEP's Executive Director, Mostafa Tolba, we are losing at least 25 million metric tons of topsoil per year.[39] Soil erosion in Africa and South America is proceeding at an annual rate of about seven tons per hectare, compared with only 0.8 tons per hectare in Europe.[40] Overall, according to Tolba, world agriculture will see a net loss of about 55 million hectares of agricultural land by the year 2000, chiefly due to erosion and desertification.[41]

Salinization or waterlogging of irrigated lands, acidification of tropical soils (intensified by the application of nitrogen fertilizers[42]), and soil compaction by heavy machinery or livestock take a further toll on soil. The reasons behind the widespread mismanagement of soil in-

Table 4. Magnitudes of annual soil erosion (tons/hectare)

Site	Forest land	Cultivated land	Bare soil
Oagadougou, Burkina Faso	0.1	0.6–8.0	10–20
Sofa, Senegal	0.2	7.3	21
Bouaké, Senegal	0.1	0.1–26	18–30
Abidjan, Ivory Coast	0.03	0.3–90	108–170

Source: P.A. Sanchez, *Properties and Management of Soils in the Tropics.*

clude population pressures and the expansion of agriculture to marginal lands. But the misapplication of technology is a major contributor.

Pests of agricultural crops—insects, pathogens, weeds, nematodes, rodents, and other organisms—also constrain crop production in the tropics. Preharvest losses due to pests run to an estimated 35 to 50 percent in some areas.[43] Agriculture in many tropical areas is especially vulnerable to pest attack, since favorable temperature and humidity may allow year-round growth and reproduction. And the diversity of species in the humid tropics can mean a larger pool of potential pests for agriculture.[44] One researcher found that crops grown in the tropics could be attacked by many more species of plant pathogens than those grown in temperate areas. *(See Table 5.)* Weeds are particularly troublesome, sometimes reducing yields to zero. In Africa and Latin America, uncontrollable weeds are one of the primary reasons that swidden plots are abandoned for newly cleared land.[45]

Table 5. Number of diseases reported on crops in tropical and temperate areas

| Crop | Number of diseases | |
	Temperate zone	Tropics
Citrus	50	248
Pumpkin squash	19	111
Sweet potato	15	187
Tomato	32	278
Rice	54	500–600
Beans	52	253–280
Potato	91	175
Maize	85	125

Source: F.L. Wellman, "More Diseases on Crops in the Tropics than in the Temperate Zone, *Ceiba* 14 (1968): 17–28.

Chemical pesticides have long been the principal means of insect control. Diseases have been controlled with both pesticides and resistant plant varieties. In contrast, weed control until recently has depended mostly on cultivation, but herbicides are now by far the largest-selling pesticides.[46]

All of these methods can pose problems. Overcultivation is a key culprit in soil erosion and desertification,[47] and it can also lead to the establishment of unproductive areas such as the *Imperata*-dominated grassland described earlier.[48] Weeding can also account for half of all the labor involved in producing a crop in developing areas. Where land is cultivated by machines, large quantities of fossil fuels are needed. While pest-resistant plant varieties effectively reduce damage from insects and diseases,[49] overreliance on host-plant resistance can lead to serious failures. Indonesia, for example, lost over two million tons of its rice crop in 1977 when the widely planted IR36 variety—introduced to combat the brown planthopper—proved susceptible to tungro virus. In part, both of these problems arose because farmers planted large areas to the same genetic type: IR36 still occupied over half of Java's lowland paddy area in 1980.[50] Rather than devise strategies to stabilize or counter evolution in pest species, plant breeders and pesticide developers alike have often tried to stay "one step ahead" of the pests—an approach that can seriously disrupt food production from time to time.

Among those concerned with the environmental effects of agriculture, pesticides have been the major focal point. Although no irrefutable numbers exist, as many as 400,000 illnesses and 10,000 deaths may be caused by pesticides every year worldwide—most of them in the developing world.[51] Resistance to pesticides, especially in insects, threatens many crops. In Malaysia, the diamondback moth is resistant to virtually all available insecticides, threatening cabbage production. Eleven species of rice-eating insect pests have shown resistance to one or more pesticide types, creating problems in Southeast Asia and elsewhere. Fungicide resistance in plant pathogens and herbicide resistance in weeds can also cause local or regional crop losses. The continuing spread of resistance—especially since fewer and fewer new types of pesticides are being discovered and marketed by the chemical industry—raises questions about the future stability of chemical-based pest control in industrialized and developing countries alike.[52]

Pest populations can be managed effectively. In industrialized countries and on commercial farms in developing countries, improving pest management calls for enhancing the support system—research, advice, and regulation—for helping farmers make sophisticated pest-control decisions.[53] For subsistence and other cash-poor farmers, new strategies will have to be developed, based primarily on traditional agricultural systems.[54] These strategies will depend less on chemicals or implements and more on the structure of the agroecosystem and other natural forces that can keep potential pests in check.

Agriculture in the tropics must not only avoid problems, but must also actively restore degraded natural resources. In agricultural development, resource utilization—soil nutrients, energy, land, and water—must be more efficient than industrialized nations' agriculture has been for some decades. And the lack of funds for industrially based inputs means that indigenous—preferably renewable—resources will be the mainstay of Third World agriculture in the future. Merely copying technologies from the industrialized world will not suffice where economic and social conditions, climate, topography, and the ecology of agricultural systems differ so radically from those in temperate zones. To succeed, the next generation of tropical agricultural systems must be built on sound ecological principles and a concrete base of region- and locale-specific ecological knowledge.

Rather than devise strategies to stabilize or counter evolution in pest species, plant breeders and pesticide developers alike have often tried to stay "one step ahead" of the pests—an approach that can seriously disrupt food production from time to time.

15

III. Ecological Paradigms and Principles for Agriculture

As part of the "modernization" of rice production in Sri Lanka, tractors have been replacing water buffaloes as the principal means of power for plowing, tilling, and threshing.[55] On the surface, the conversion seemed to make sense, saving eight to nine worker days per acre. But look closer.

Economically, using tractors increased costs to farmers when fuel prices skyrocketed in the 1970s. Indirect costs also abound. To begin, the buffalo long provided milk and curd for the farm family—items that now have to be purchased. In addition, buffalo dung and urine were used to fertilize fields; now, store-bought inorganic fertilizers have to be used instead. Also, buffalo herding is a source of employment for young villagers, so income is lost if tractors replace buffaloes.

Other costs associated with replacing the buffalo are more subtle. Tractors disrupt the soil structure that was partially created by the buffaloes' trampling, so water retention and yields are down. And removing the pools that were kept as buffalo wallows in the rice fields has had unexpected and serious consequences:

> As the rice fields dry out completely during the harvest season, the majority of their aquatic fauna die out. The recolonization of the fields is usually achieved during flood times by organisms that have maintained their populations in 'drought refugia,' habitats which contain water through the dry period such as rivers or lakes. The greater the distance from a drought [refuge] to a given field, the smaller the likelihood of it being recolonized.... The buffalo wallows also function as very efficient drought refugia for aquatic organisms and ensure the recolonization of the set of fields associated with them after the dry season....[56]

Many ecological benefits have disappeared with the wallows. Edible fish harvested in drought refugia run as high as 350 to 400 pounds per acre. Mosquito-eating fish that lived in the wallows helped control malaria-carrying mosquitoes, so now more insecticides have to be used to control malaria. Two other beneficial species that depend on the wallows area as a breeding ground are the rat snake and the lizard *Varanus salvator:* the snake is an important predator of rats and mice that would otherwise eat ripening grain in the fields, while the lizard consumes fresh-water crabs whose burrows weaken and destroy the rice-field bunds necessary for good water management. These wallows also supply water for soaking the coconut branches used in thatched roofs. If thatch is unavailable and replaced by roofing tiles (which have to be fired), firewood demand will increase and so will the already high deforestation rate.

The ecological linkages in this small example of a changing production system show the need to think much more clearly about proposed technological "improvements." Most traditional farming systems have evolved over centuries, even millenia, and the natural world has evolved along with them. The coevolution of wild animals and plants with agricultural activities can affect how whole farming systems function, and any change should be undertaken with care. Such change must be based on a clearer understanding of the ecological structure and function of agroecosystems if agriculture is to become more sustainable and productive.

The Meanings of Sustainability

Just what is a sustainable agriculture? California economist Gordon Douglass points out that "sustainability" has different meanings for different schools of thought:

- The "food-sufficiency" or "productivity" viewpoint, which "thinks of sustainability as supplying enough food to meet everyone's demand";
- The "stewardship" school, which "regards sustainability primarily as an ecological phenomenon," with a concern for maintaining an "average level of output over an indefinitely long period...without depleting the renewable resources on which it depends"; and
- The "community" perspective, which "pays most attention to the effects of different agricultural systems on the vitality, social organization, and culture of rural life."[57]

Since neither productivity nor rural life can be maintained if production systems are not ecologically stable in the long term, a definition of sustainability—like the stewardship school's objectives—must be based on the resources underlying production and on the means for conserving them. Stephen Gliessman, director of the agroecology program at the University of California at Santa Cruz, describes this orientation toward "average level of output" as seeking to "optimize productivity on a long-term basis rather than maximize it on the short term."[58] Indeed, to be maintained over an "indefinitely long period," agricultural systems must be capable of continuous, reliable production levels—akin to the idea of optimum sustainable yield in wildlife management.[59] (An older concept of maximum sustainable yield originated with fisheries scientists who sought to set fish catches at the level where the harvest would equal the maximum calculated population replacement rate, so that the harvest could be taken essentially forever.[60] Unfortunately, harvest rates were calculated as though single species were in isolation from their environment. Other factors

To be maintained over an "indefinitely long period," agricultural systems must be capable of continuous, reliable production levels—akin to the idea of optimum sustainable yield in wildlife management.

in the ecosystem that interact with the species in question would in-evitably cause the system to collapse. The new approach uses a more realistic model of population dynamics, taking into account inter-actions among species and between organisms and the environment.)

With agriculture, different kinds of replacement rates, including those concerning soil nutrients and organic matter, water, and various beneficial plant and animal species, come into play. Thus, Douglass' third criterion is essential: that renewable resources not be depleted.

Soil scientist D.J. Greenland of the International Rice Research In-stitute describes more concretely the conditions necessary for a stable agriculture:

1. The chemical nutrients removed by crops are replenished in the soil;
2. The physical condition of the soil suited to the land utilization type is maintained, which usually means that the humus level in the soil is constant or increasing;
3. There is no build-up of weeds, pests, and diseases;
4. There is no increase in soil acidity or of toxic elements; and
5. Soil erosion is controlled.[61]

Greenland's criteria refer primarily to the production site or farm level. To these must be added the obvious requirements that farming must be productive and profitable.

The field and farm are but the first two levels in the organizational hierarchy that define agroecosystems.[62] Looked at on a regional (multi-farm) level, sustainability takes on new dimensions, including the need to:

1. Minimize dependence on nonrenewable energy, mineral, and chemical resources;[63]
2. Reduce off-farm contamination of air, water, and land by nutrients and toxic materials to levels at which self-cleansing is continually possible;
3. Maintain adequate habitat for wildlife; and
4. Conserve genetic resources in plant and animal species needed for agriculture.

At the national and international levels, the productivity and com-munity definitions from Douglass' typology are more predominant: people need food and income, import costs must be minimized, and unique ecosystems need to be preserved. If agriculture can be stabi-lized at the field, farm, and regional levels, the concerns farther up the hierarchy can be addressed effectively. Conversely, if sustainability is not attained at the lowest level, it will be impossible at higher levels. What is needed is a new long-term program in agricultural research, development, and implementation that is oriented toward system design rather than piecemeal modifications.

Ecology: The Integrative Science

Just as groups of people show distinct behaviors that sociologists, economists, political scientists, and others analyze, natural systems (groups of plants, animals, and microbes) display collective characteristics that differ from a simple sum of the individual actions of the group members. Exactly what happens when organisms interact with each other and with the nonliving environment (including weather) is the subject of ecology, a science defined by Charles Krebs of the University of British Columbia as the "study of the interactions that determine the distribution and abundance of organisms."[64] Ecology is also concerned with changes in distribution and abundance over time—essential for understanding the stability of natural systems and the sustainability of managed ones such as agriculture.

Ecologists generally study three levels of organization: populations, communities, and ecosystems. *Populations* are groups of organisms belonging to the same species, generally occupying a contiguous area and characterized by reproduction or birth rates, mortality rates, and immigration and emigration rates. These processes interact, creating identifiable age structures in populations. Taken together, these attributes define population growth and decline, and they help determine where populations are located and when.

In nature, no species exists in isolation from all others, but rather in complex associations called *communities*—the collection of populations in a given place and the relationships among them. The interactions among its members define a community's attributes. These include the species composition (Which species are present in the community and in what numbers?) and the food web, or trophic structure (Which species eat which other species?). In a process known as *succession*, many communities gradually change: some species are displaced by others and new species are added to the system. Species diversity— expressed as the number of species or the relative numerical importance of the various species—is often used to describe the differences in structure and evolutionary "maturity" among communities.[65] The dynamics of communities (expressed in terms of energy and nutrient flows through the food web and the rate of change in species composition) are determined by rates of primary (photosynthetic) production and consumption by herbivores, carnivores, and decomposers. Just as natural populations exist only in association with others, the fate of living and nonliving components are intricately bound together.

In each case the community has a close-linked, interacting relation to environment, as climate and soil affect the community and the community affects the soil and its own internal climate or microclimate, as energy and matter are taken from environment to run the community's living function and its substance, transferred from one organism to another in the community, and released back to environment. A community and its environment treated together as a functional system of complementary relationships, and transfer and circulation of energy and matter, is an ecosystem.[66]

Because it best encompasses the most significant physical and biotic relationships that affect organisms, the ecosystem has often been described as the basic unit of ecology.[67] Like the community, its characteristics are determined by nutrient and energy flows, species composition and diversity, trophic structure, and rates of production, consumption, and decomposition. The difference is that in an ecosystem the nonliving stores and sources of materials and energy are considered along with the animals, plants, and microbes that inhabit the environment.

Ecosystem Development

Understanding the evolution of communities and ecosystems is particularly important for identifying the ecological conditions that must underlie sustainable agriculture. Because of the ways in which human beings change the environment when they grow crops, agriculture usually shares many of the characteristics of "immature" ecosystems in nature.

In the 1960s, ecologists Ramon Margalef and Eugene Odum devised similar theories to describe the changes that occur as ecosystems develop.[68] In Margalef's terms, ecosystem maturity increases with time in undisturbed ecosystems, and mature systems differ markedly from ecosystems at earlier stages of development in terms of increases in biomass (living matter), species diversity, and stratification (such as the larger number of leaf canopy layers in a mature forest) or spatial heterogeneity. Trophic structures in mature systems are longer and more complex than in immature ones, according to Margalef and Odum. In general, later stages of ecosystem development are characterized by a higher degree of organization or community structure than earlier stages.

Energy flow in different types of ecosystems may be especially significant for the design of future agricultural systems. Both Margalef and Odum note the relationship of primary productivity—the capture of solar energy by plants and the resultant production of biomass—to the amount of biomass in the community (sometimes called the "standing crop"). The ratio of productivity to biomass decreases with increasing maturity, and, Odum further notes, productivity comes to approximately equal respiration—the rate of using up the captured energy—as ecosystems mature. Thus, in mature ecosystems, energy is used principally to maintain the system rather than to add new material. In contrast, less mature ecosystems have high production-to-biomass ratios and living matter accumulates. These conditions, Margalef points out, favor the exploitation of immature ecosystems rather than mature ones. Agriculture has often been described as artificially maintaining a site at an early successional stage (low maturity) to exploit the high net productivity (accumulating biomass) rather than letting the system progress to later stages.

One cost of keeping an ecosystem immature is that nutrient cycling is "open" rather than "closed." This means that essential minerals

Agriculture has often been described as artificially maintaining a site at an early successional stage (low maturity) to exploit the high net productivity (accumulating biomass) rather than letting the system progress to later stages.

and other nutrients do not readily stay in the system, but "leak" out, sometimes at high rates. In a deforested site in New Hampshire, for example, mineral nutrient levels in stream runoff were three to fifteen times higher than in similar areas where the forest was left standing.[69] As ecosystems mature, says Odum, the cycling of such elements as nitrogen and calcium is "tightened" as the system becomes better at trapping and holding nutrients and at passing them slowly from one organism to another.

Where immature ecosystems are economically exploited, it must be remembered that the natural forces that help stabilize ecosystems and communities are typically more characteristic of *mature* systems. According to Margalef, population fluctuations are more pronounced in immature ecosystems than in mature ones, and the mechanisms that control population size in early stages of ecosystem development are more likely to be physical (such as weather) rather than biological (such as predators or food supply). Finely tuned controls on population numbers are more feasible with biological forces than with physical constraints, since the latter tend to vary randomly. According to both theorists, the types of organisms in mature and immature ecosystems differ. Early stages of development are dominated by species that tend to have short life spans, exhibit broad food and habitat preferences, and are geared toward rapid population increase—sometimes referred to as "pioneer" or "opportunistic" species. Many agricultural pests fall into this category. They are adapted to exploit newly opened habitats, and early successional stages, whether natural or artificial (such as regularly cleared fields), are ideal for them. Organisms in mature ecosystems tend toward longer life spans, have more specialized food and habitat needs, and are oriented toward living with their neighbors through cooperation or dividing available resources. Moreover, Odum defines the "strategy" of ecosystem development as tending toward "increasing control of, or homeostasis with, the physical environment in the sense of achieving maximum protection from its perturbations." Taken as a whole, these observations point to an important constraint on agriculture: trying to achieve maximum stability of a complex biomass structure often conflicts with efforts to obtain the highest yield.[70]

Margalef's and Odum's theories have potentially valuable insights for the development of sustainable agriculture. In particular, the concepts of ecosystem maturity and ecosystem development could point the direction for future strategies in agroecosystem design and management. For example, Robert Hart of the Winrock International Institute for Agricultural Development has suggested an "analog" approach to food production systems, wherein an agricultural site would be managed so as to mimic natural succession.[71] Beginning with annual grasses and broad-leaved species, such as maize and beans, Hart's proposed system progresses through stages of plantings to a "forest" of economically valuable trees and understory crops with many of the ecological characteristics of a maturing tropical rain forest. *(See Figure 1.)* The highly diverse and productive home-gardens of Java

Trying to achieve maximum stability of a complex biomass structure often conflicts with efforts to obtain the highest yield.

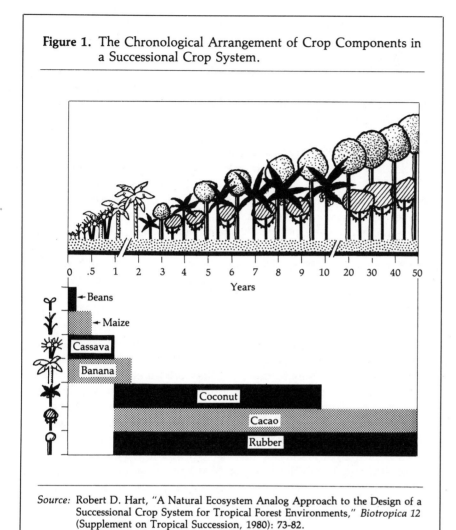

Figure 1. The Chronological Arrangement of Crop Components in a Successional Crop System.

Source: Robert D. Hart, "A Natural Ecosystem Analog Approach to the Design of a Successional Crop System for Tropical Forest Environments," *Biotropica 12* (Supplement on Tropical Succession, 1980): 73-82.

exemplify a traditional system that uses this strategy: as in natural succession, each stage creates the physical conditions (such as light and shade and soil organic matter) needed by the next.[72] Hart's approach—directing succession rather than fighting it—could alleviate the unending battle against weeds so characteristic of annual cropping systems, and reduce the energy and labor costs of establishing perennial crops. The result would be an evolving agricultural system with increasing diversity and reduced susceptibility to disruption.

Diversity and Stability

The diversity of species in natural habitats has long fascinated ecologists, especially those trying to explain why some communities have larger numbers of species while others have fewer.[73] Of particular importance to agriculture has been the oft-repeated claim that diversity causes, enhances, or otherwise contributes to stability. At various times, the diversity-stability relationship has been described by highly respected biologists as a rule, a principle, an ''immutable law,'' and as ''proven beyond doubt.''[74] Although by the 1960s the diversity-stability connection was widely touted, especially by conservationists, the hypothesis was based on some anecdotal evidence and a brief theoretical analysis.[75]

The diversity-stability hypothesis has intuitive appeal, going back to the Social Darwinists of the 19th century and undoubtedly to folk wisdom about eggs and baskets.[76] If true, it provides a strong practical argument for conservation—for maintaining diversity in ecosystems whenever possible as a natural buffer against perturbation.[77] But if the theory is flawed, basing policies upon it could have unexpected and undesirable environmental consequences. For instance, if diversity causes stability, the most species-rich communities—such as tropical rain forests and coral reefs—should be able to withstand the greatest disruption at human hands. In fact, these communities are among the most fragile.[78]

Today, the experimental evidence[78] and theoretical analysis[80] reveal the notion that diversity causes stability as oversimplified at best, if not dead wrong. As an explanation for the differences in diversity, the hypothesis has given way to more sophisticated ideas of environmental predictability, population adaptation, and coevolution among species, leading to increased specialization and symbiotic relations.[81] And both data and theory are pointing more to the characteristics of particular population interactions as determining stability: a ''qualitative'' view of the causes of stability as opposed to a ''quantitative'' view that simply counts the number of species to predict stability.[82] The implications for agriculture are far-reaching. The qualitative basis of stability means that agricultural ecosystems cannot be made more stable simply by increasing complexity. Instead, the interactions that occur in agroecosystems must be carefully evaluated to determine the stabilizing and destabilizing elements and to design systems accordingly.

A major shortcoming of early thinking about diversity and stability was that, although considerable effort went into defining the former both conceptually and operationally, the meaning of stability was not rigorously examined.[83] In fact, stability has several connotations, each important. Margalef drew one key distinction: ''adjustment'' *vs.* ''persistence.'' He described adjustment in these terms: ''a system is stable if, when changed from a steady state, it develops forces that tend to restore it to its original condition.''[84] (This is the ''homeostasis'' in Odum's theory of ecosystem development, though ''resilience'' is the most descriptive term.[85]) According to Margalef, a system is persistent ''if it remains much the same and [even if] its presumed stability [resilience] is never tested,'' that is, by disturbing it from its steady state.[86] A third aspect of stability is described by Canadian ecologist

If diversity causes stability, the most species-rich communities—such as tropical rain forests and coral reefs—should be able to withstand the greatest disruption at human hands. In fact, these communities are among the most fragile.

C.S. Holling as "the ability of...systems to absorb changes...and still persist."[87] (This property might best be given the name "resistance," the ecosystem's tendency to retain its character in the face of disturbance.) Hence, stability has two dimensions—time and disturbance. Persistence is the tendency of the system to look the same through time, resistance is its capacity to withstand disturbance, and resilience is its ability to recover if the disturbance causes change.[88]

Two other distinctions round out the concept of stability. The first is the difference between local or neighborhood stability and global stability.[89] Global stability indicates that, no matter how much a system is changed from its original state (for instance, a particular species mix), it will revert to that state given enough time. Local stability means that the system will return to its original state unless change is too great, in which case it may find itself in another persistent state. In practical terms, and probably even in theory, only local stability is relevant since it is always possible to imagine a disturbance so severe that an ecosystem cannot naturally appear in its original form again. Consider desertification: in many parts of the world, simply putting a stop to destructive practices won't restore the land to its earlier state; instead, massive regeneration efforts are required.

Another important distinction is that between stability as an equilibrium versus stability as a changeable state. Although ecologists have constructed many population models around the notion of equilibrium points, Princeton scientist Robert May believes that nature is more accurately represented as having "stable limit cycles" in which the state of the community changes in some regular pattern, be they seasons or longer-term oscillations.[90] An even more "permissive" view of stability would have the ecosystem change state within some boundaries, but not necessarily with any regularity. The latter probably most readily approximates nature, since random shifts are to be expected in any ecosystem at least partially affected by such variables as temperature and rainfall.

Making practical use of the concept of stability in designing and managing sustainable agricultural systems requires taking these distinctions to heart and developing realistic expectations for agroecosystem stability. Increasing diversity for its own sake will not necessarily improve sustainability, and poorly designed diversity may actually be destabilizing. Seeking global stability would clearly be fruitless; local stability should be the goal, and the types and severity of expected perturbations will have to be spelled out, along with the acceptable time horizons for ecosystem response and recovery. Certainly, persistence of agroecosystem structure and function is desirable and necessary, most readily defined as the minimization of variation in output.[91] And resistance to disturbances should be built into all agricultural systems. Fluctuations in pest numbers, climatic conditions, and water availability will have to be taken into account when plant and animal varieties are selected, crop mixes designed, and management strategies developed. Anticipating hurricanes, floods, and other major perturbations will mean planning structural resistance in the form of windbreaks, terraces, and other landscape features to minimize the effect of these events. And if change does occur, the system must be capable of rapid recovery.[92] All of these goals point to the need for carefully designed agroecosystems. Not only will ecosystem and community structure have to be considered in detail when designing these systems, but also the characteristics of, and relationships among, component populations.

Population Concepts: Dynamics and Interactions

The growth, maintenance, and decline of population numbers stems from the interplay of various factors—some more or less inherent to the species, but most dependent on how populations of species in the community affect each other. Each species' reproductive rate differs, depending on the ages at which reproduction commences and ends, the number of individuals at each age, the number of offspring produced at each age, and the likely survival of offspring. Under optimal conditions, these characteristics together define a species' ''intrinsic rate of natural increase.''[93] Under the right conditions, species with high rates of increase can exploit newly opened habitats better than species with lower rates of increase. For instance, annual weeds are the first plants to populate cleared fields and, because they produce so many seeds, they can quickly dominate the landscape unless farmers plow or otherwise intervene.

As populations increase in number over time, they often begin to saturate the available habitable space, use up the food supply, or otherwise crowd each other out. Population growth in these circumstances then slows and can eventually reach some level above which growth cannot be sustained. This theoretical environmental limit to population size, or ''carrying capacity,'' has been demonstrated in laboratory populations.[94] Its precise applicability to the natural world is open to debate, but the environment undoubtedly imposes some upper limit for any population, and the dynamics of populations at or near the carrying capacity differ from those well below it. For instance, reproduction at the carrying capacity is not at the maximum possible rate but only at a rate roughly equal to the death rate.

How important is the concept of carrying capacity for agriculture? Does it imply inherent limits to productivity, or can technology overcome any barriers? The answers to these questions are not simple. To begin with, not all populations exhibit growth curves with characteristic carrying capacities. Odum distinguishes two basic types of population growth patterns: a ''J''-shaped curve in which growth proceeds at the maximum rate until environmental conditions change and the population ''crashes,'' and an ''S''-shaped curve in which growth gradually slows as the carrying capacity is reached and the population numbers then hover about that level. Particular population growth patterns can vary considerably from these two ideal types, sometimes following one or the other or some combination of the two as conditions change.[95] And conditions *do* change: constant environments are rare in nature, if they exist at all. Hence, the environment may be able to sustain one population level in one season and a lower or higher one in another season. Weather, for example, can influence reproduction, survival, the food supply, and the relative importance of predators and competitors. The movement of species in and out of particular habitats can also affect how many members of other species can survive in those areas. In short, the maximum allowable population can vary in both time and space in innumerable ways. Trying to calculate that maximum as if it were an absolute number would be futile.

As applied to agriculture, the concept of carrying capacity must include even more variables—witness the methodological and conceptual difficulties faced by anthropologists who have tried to calculate carrying capacities for agricultural populations.[96] To assess what agricultural production levels the environment will allow, we would have to specify what technologies are being used, what new technologies could be applied, and the environmental impact of each technique in the short and long terms. Instead of assigning some *a priori* maximum to the expected capacity of a particular site to produce food, it makes more sense to examine the productivity and stability—resilience, resistance, and persistence—of specific production systems, including site characteristics and technologies.

Ecologists have described ways that species have evolved different adaptations at two ends of an environmental spectrum: some species exploit ''open'' habitats through invasion and high reproduction, while others specialize in living under ''saturated'' environments by competing effectively for limited resources.[97] The first—a productivity ''strategy''—stresses filling the environment; the second—an efficiency strategy—emphasizes staying in it. The first is expected to be favored where physical environments are highly variable and unpredictable, mortality factors are little affected by the population density, and competition from other species for resources is slight. The second would more likely emerge where climates are fairly predictable, mortality factors are affected strongly by population levels, and the environment is keenly competitive.[98] In designing sustainable agricultural systems, researchers need to look at both kinds of adaptations and determine when and where each fits: productivity strategies for the necessary increases in food availability, and efficiency strategies for the needed stability.

Often, the growth and decline of a population depends on interactions with other species. One species feeds on another, each helping to regulate the other's numbers. Two or more species may compete for the same resource, be it nesting sites or food supply or light, and thus limit each other's population to levels below what they might be in the absence of competition. Symbiotic relationships evolve where two species, rather than competing, cooperate. Each of these processes can add to or detract from a community's stability, depending on the precise nature and extent of the interaction. Predation can maintain diversity in an ecosystem by preventing any one species

Instead of assigning some **a priori** *maximum to the expected capacity of a particular site to produce food, it makes more sense to examine the productivity and stability—resilience, resistance, and persistence—of specific production systems.*

from dominating the landscape, but invading predators can seriously upset the balance of a community by disrupting the ecological forces that keep species' numbers in check. Competitors can share their common resource in some way, or one species can drive another to local extinction. Strong mutual dependence can mean high persistence of associated species within a community, but the entire group of species may disappear if something disrupts any component population.

Some ecologists have used the terminology and concepts of cybernetics to understand the stabilizing and destabilizing properties of communities and ecosystems.[99] One key here is the self-correcting "negative feedback loop"—best illustrated by a thermostat. If the temperature falls below or rises above a set point, the heating system is turned on or off to bring the temperature back to the desired level. Similarly, a predator can efficiently regulate a prey population by increasing its feeding rate and its numbers when prey numbers go up, and "easing up" as the prey population declines (and prey become harder to find).[100] Studies of the dynamics of predator-prey and parasite-host systems have been especially valuable in understanding how to design stable biological pest-control programs. (Other negative feedback loops in agroecosystems might include plants' growing faster or producing toxins in response to insect damage, or ecosystems' changing their rate of nutrient cycling in response to fertilization.) In contrast, positive feedback, whereby change is accelerated rather than restrained by the interactions in an ecosystem, is destabilizing—witness desertification. Once started, a desert often creates the conditions for its own expansion.

Competition among plants and animals for life-giving resources can be a major factor in determining various species' distribution and abundance. Taking a page from ecologists who have sought to understand how species coexist in communities, agriculturists may learn how to create environments that take advantage of competitors' tendency to share a habitat by subdividing it.[101] Time and again, ecological studies of agriculture have shown that mixtures of carefully selected plants use light, water, and nutrients more efficiently than do single-species plantings.

Another very important feature of species in the natural world is their capacity for evolution. Most populations comprise a wide array of genetically unique individuals, some of which are likely to survive as environmental conditions change. Modern agriculture has learned the risks of removing that genetic diversity from plant populations: plant diseases have wiped out large areas of genetically uniform crops, leading to severe economic loss and human suffering. Traditional farming practices have for the most part preserved genetic diversity and directed the evolution of crop plants to meet specific ecological conditions, nutritional needs, and individual tastes. Only recently have agricultural scientists begun to examine the relevance of natural genetic diversity and apply that knowledge to cropping systems.[102]

The natural world is incredibly diverse and complex, and its multitudinous structures and processes cannot be pigeonholed into a few

The natural world's multitudinous structures and processes cannot be pigeonholed into a few universal principles.

28

universal principles. The concept of community, for instance, may sometimes be more heuristic than real, with temporal and spatial shifts in species composition occurring often and unpredictably. Hence, stability can be difficult to measure. And communities may not always evolve according to theory. Although order and constancy appear everywhere in nature, so do disorder and change, and not everything that occurs can be readily explained by existing concepts. Most important, ecology attempts to explain, not prescribe.[103] If sustainability is made a goal of agriculture, ecologists' insights can be incorporated in agroecosystems to meet that goal. Alternatively, if sustainability is ignored, ecologists may be able to predict some of the consequences. But the choice between the two paths is a social one influenced by such factors as short-term nutritional and monetary needs, energy and materials costs, alternative development strategies, and questions of economic and political equity and power. Policymakers must make these decisions based on all of these considerations, but they must also remember that, however they choose, their actions will evoke responses from nature. Some of those responses will benefit people in expected and desirable ways. But if the unexpected is to be avoided, planning based on ecological principles is needed to keep development hopes from being dashed by environmental degradation and resource depletion.

Ecology attempts to explain, not prescribe.

29

IV. Applications of Ecological Concepts to Agriculture

Just as the ecosystem is a key organizational unit in ecology, the agroecosystem—though at once simpler and more complex than its "natural" counterpart—is the parallel unit in the study of agriculture. Agroecosystems are simpler in that they usually contain fewer species than their nearest natural analog. Compare, for instance, a ricefield and a marsh, or a wheat field and a grassland community. But human intervention also makes agroecosystems more ecologically complex. Natural ecosystems are for the most part internally regulated: their energy and nutrient flows, the species composition and population densities are determined primarily by the interactions of the various biological and physical components within the system. On the other hand, human activity is a principal determinant of many, if not most, of an agroecosystem's characteristics.

A key to differentiating the two kinds of ecosystems is the energy flow. Not just sunlight, but also energy directed by people plays an enormous role in the dynamics of agroecosystems, determining nutrient levels and flow directions, raising or lowering plant and animal population densities, removing biomass from the ecosystem as harvested crops, and directing (or arresting) the course of ecosystem evolution. In aboriginal agricultural systems, the principal sources of energy are human and animal power, and, especially in swidden agriculture, fire. All of these sources derive their energy from the photosynthetic activities of plants, however near or remote from the site of production. And all but the most isolated agriculturists use some fossil fuels (or products made with their help). In contrast, many technologically advanced agricultural systems are so dependent on oil and gas that some actually import more energy in fuel than they export in food.[104]

By definition, an agroecosystem is an ecosystem whose structure and function have been modified by people to produce food, fiber, or other products. Narrowly defined, the agroecosystem comprises principally the biological interactions occurring at the field or farm level. Some scientists contend that the boundary between biological and human activities is blurry, and so people become part of these researchers' purview in defining the agroecosystem.[105] Other analysts believe that the farm or field is too small a geographic unit to contain all relevant interactions and that the agroecosystem is better thought of as comprising regions as large as an entire nation or subcontinent.[106]

Increasingly, the concept of the agroecosystem is helping some scientists and agricultural development specialists understand and, eventually, design sustainable production systems. Their work points to some important new directions for world agriculture.

Analysis and Design of Polyculture Systems

One hallmark of industrialized agriculture has been an ever-increasing reliance on monocultures. Monoculture—growing one crop on the same land year after year—often gives the large-scale commercial farmer an edge in marketing, mechanization, and other economic efficiencies. For certain crops, there may be some biological benefits as well—among them, control of some plant diseases. But as a general model of food production, monoculture raises some troubling questions. The high degree of farm-level and regional specialization leaves farmers vulnerable to price fluctuations, pest outbreaks, and weather. Nutrient-demanding crops in monoculture deplete natural soil fertility and lead to greater dependence on purchased fertilizers. Many monoculture systems leave soil exposed to wind and water erosion during part of the year. And, while these systems may save labor and cash, many use energy and land inefficiently.

In studies of tropical agriculture, a recurrent theme is the prevalence of farming systems employing more than one crop—in sequence, in combination, or both—and mixing crop and animal production units in complex, interrelated systems. In Africa, 98 percent of all cowpeas—the continent's most important legume—are grown in combination with other crops. A 1974 survey in northern Nigeria found over 80 percent of the cropland planted to mixed-crop systems. In Latin America, beans are grown with maize, potatoes, and other crops, accounting for 90 percent of bean production in Colombia, 73 percent in Guatemala, and 80 percent in Brazil. Maize is planted with other crops on about 60 percent of tropical Latin America's maize-growing area.[107] These systems, once regarded as primitive, are actually the result of years of cultural evolution, and they reflect intimate knowledge of the farm site and the interactions taking place there. Where most scientists used to look for ways to supplant indigenous farming systems with high-technology, capital- and energy-intensive production systems originating in the industrialized countries, some now study the old ways, looking to improve certain elements that can be improved without losing the integrity of the whole.

A prime example of the richness of information and inherent good sense found in traditional polycultures is the Javanese home-garden of Indonesia.[108] Studies of these small but highly productive plots—accounting for 2.25 million hectares, or 17 percent of the country's agricultural land—show that their ecological characteristics resemble those of natural forests. Gardens are planted with mixtures of perennial and annual species in incredibly rich assemblages: in one survey

In one survey of 351 Javanese home-gardens, researchers recorded 607 plant species, with an overall species diversity comparable to deciduous subtropical forests.

of 351 Javanese home-gardens, researchers recorded 607 plant species, with an overall species diversity comparable to deciduous subtropical forests. Plants are organized vertically as well as horizontally in the garden to take advantage of all available sunlight. At least four distinct canopy layers have been identified, from coffee and guava at the top to herbs and shrubs in the bottom. Together, the layers intercept as much as 99.75 percent of the sunlight, thanks to knowledgeable gardeners who match species and sites with the plants' light requirements in mind. Moreover, since the diverse plant assemblages rarely leave the soil uncovered, soil erosion is barely noticeable.[109]

In Africa, too, the mixed-crop system, in some of its forms, exhibits a "riotous physiognomy, [and] bears a strong affinity to the forest from which it was originally carved."[110] A typical farm in Nigeria might contain upwards of eight crops, including bananas, beans, cassava, melons, and yams, as well as a scattering of other species. Farm yield per acre is high, as is the overall leaf area per unit area of ground.[111]

Agricultural scientists have begun to examine crop mixtures to discern the reasons behind polyculture's popularity and success. Australian agronomist B.R. Trenbath's review of 572 experiments on plant mixtures found that in about 20 percent of the studies, mixtures produce more than monocultures.[112] (See Figure 2.) As Stephen Gliessman has pointed out, most of the cases that Trenbath examined were experimental, and a sampling based on mixed-crop systems used widely might very well show a larger proportion with relatively higher total yields. But even the probably conservative 20 percent figure demonstrates the need to take greater advantage of those crop combinations that improve performance.[113] According to Trenbath, mixtures perform better when species complement one another as to growth rhythms, rooting depths, and use of nutrients and light.[114]

Several of these factors can be at work in any given situation. Javanese home-gardens clearly benefit from efficient light utilization. In Trinidad, intercropping maize and pigeon peas increased the efficiency of nutrient uptake, perhaps because the component species had differing nutritional requirements and discrete root layers.[115] Relative yield totals of 1.54 and 1.78 for mixed and row intercrops, respectively, indicated the productive advantage of the polyculture. Equally important, the polyculture took up from 1.3 to 2.0 times as much nutrients from the soil as the monoculture did, making much more complete use of available resources. (See Table 6.)

In Mexico, Gliessman and his colleagues have been comparing traditional crop mixtures, using the land equivalent ratio (LER), which is the relative amount of land planted in monoculture that would be needed to achieve the same yield as a mixture. They found that 1.73 hectares of land would have to be planted in maize to produce as much food as one hectare planted to a mixture of maize, beans, and squash. If total biomass (as opposed to just food) is compared, the mixture is even more advantageous. (See Table 7.) Since most of the noncrop biomass is plowed back into the soil or fed to animals whose

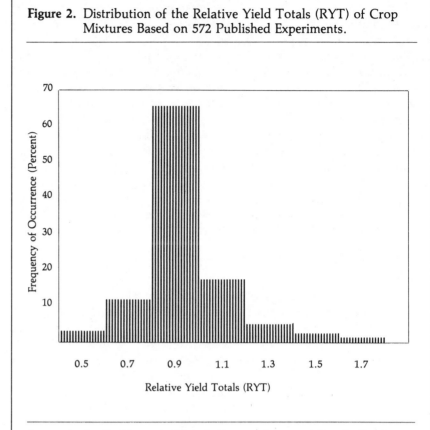

Figure 2. Distribution of the Relative Yield Totals (RYT) of Crop Mixtures Based on 572 Published Experiments.

Source: Stephen R. Gliessman, "Multiple Cropping Systems: A Basis for Developing an Alternative Agriculture" based on data from B.R. Trenbath, "Biomass Productivity of Mixtures," *Advances in Agronomy 26* (1974): 177-210.

dung is used as fertilizer, this added benefit of the mixture—increasing the total organic matter in the soil—is a key to the long-term mainten- ance of the agroecosystem. Another Mexican study found that a maize-bean polyculture produced almost four tons of dry matter per hectare for re-incorporation, compared to 2.3 tons per hectare in a maize monoculture.[116]

Mixed cropping has also been found advantageous in experimental work in Africa and Asia. In Cameroon, total yields of a mixture of maize and groundnuts were 21 and 11 percent higher, respectively, for unfertilized and fertilized mixtures than for maize monocultures receiving the same fertility regime. Land equivalent ratios ranged from 1.24 to 1.34 in the unfertilized mixtures, and from 1.17 to 1.49 in the fertilized areas. (The differences between fertilized and unfertilized plots suggests that nitrogen availability was probably a limiting factor in production.)[117] In Indonesia, an intercropping system—planting rice and maize at the same time, followed by cassava two months later

Table 6. Effects of Mixed and Row Intercropping* of Maize (M) and Pigeon Pea (PP) in St. Augustine, Trinidad, Expressed as Relative Yield Totals (RYT)

Item	Sole Crop		Mixed Intercrop			Row Intercrop		
	M	PP	M	PP	RYT	M	PP	RYT
Production (t./ha.):								
Grain yield	3.1	1.9	2.0	1.7	1.54	2.6	1.8	1.78
Total dry matter	6.4	5.1	4.2	3.8	1.40	5.0	4.9	1.74
Nutrient uptake (kg./ha.):								
Nitrogen	66.0	119.0	48.0	100.0	1.56	54.0	127.0	1.88
Phosphorus	13.0	6.0	9.0	5.0	1.52	11.0	7.0	2.01
Potassium	51.0	37.0	37.0	32.0	1.59	46.0	33.0	1.79
Calcium	10.0	22.0	10.0	15.0	1.68	9.0	19.0	1.76
Magnesium	12.0	14.0	9.0	8.0	1.32	9.0	12.0	1.61

*Mixed intercropping is growing two or more crops simultaneously with no distinct row arrangement. Row intercropping is growing two or more crops with one or more crops planted in rows.

Source: P.A. Sanchez, *Properties and Management of Soils in the Tropics.*

and, after the grains were harvested, legumes such as cowpeas or peanuts—was compared with a sequential planting of three crops without cassava. The intercrop produced somewhat less overall than sequential planting, but gave higher net returns. Intercropped plots receiving no lime, fertilizer, or mulch netted $219 per hectare, compared to a $14 per hectare net *loss* for sequentially planted plots similarly managed. When lime, fertilizer, and mulch were used, the differences were even more dramatic: net returns per hectare for the intercrop were $639, versus $178 for the sequential plantings.[118]

In China, some of the advantage of a rubber-tea intercrop lies in the crop residues. The residues' value was calculated in terms of the nutrients that they supply to the soil. Chinese scientists determined that the plant debris deposited on the soil provided the equivalent of 813 kilograms per hectare (kg./ha.) of ammonium sulfate (nitrogen fertilizer), 65 kg./ha. of calcium superphosphate, and 146 kg./ha. of potassium sulfate. In addition, the intercrop was estimated to have reduced soil erosion by 70 percent and raised the minimum temperature in the stand by two degrees Centigrade, thus reducing the risk of cold damage to the rubber trees. Yields were also reported to be higher than with monocultures.[119]

Table 7. Yields and Total Biomass of Maize, Beans, and Squash (kg./ha.) Planted in Polyculture as Compared to Several Densities (Plants/ha.) of Each Crop in Monoculture

Crop	Monoculture				Polyculture
Maize:					
Density	33,300	40,000	66,600	100,000	50,000
Yield	990	1,150	1,230	1,170	1,720
Biomass	2,823	3,119	4,478	4,871	5,927
Beans:					
Density	56,800	64,000	100,000	133,200	40,000
Yield	425	740	610	695	110
Biomass	853	895	843	1,390	253
Squash:					
Density	1,200	1,875	7,500	30,000	3,330
Yield	15	250	430	225	80
Biomass	241	941	1,254	802	478
TOTAL POLYCULTURE YIELD:					1,910
TOTAL POLYCULTURE BIOMASS:					6,659

Land Equivalent Ratios (LER)*
Based on yield: 1.73
Based on biomass: 1.78
* LER = sum [(yield or biomass of each crop in polyculture)/ (maximum yield or biomass of each crop in monoculture)]

Source: M.F. Amador, *Comportamiento de Tres Especies (Maiz, Frijol, Calabaza) en Policultivos en la Chontalpa, Tabasco, Mexico,* Tesis Profesional, Colegio Superior de Agricultura Tropical, Tabasco, Mexico, 1980. Cited in Gliessman, "Multiple Cropping Systems: A Basis for Developing an Alternative Agriculture."

Why is polyculture so widespread? The examples discussed above certainly support productivity and improved fertility as prime reasons for continued reliance on multiple-cropping systems. Another possible advantage of mixtures is pest control, though the evidence is far from one-sided. In Costa Rica, mixing cassava and beans reduced the incidence and severity of powdery mildew on cassava and angular leaf spot on beans but left other diseases unaffected. In a maize-bean intercrop, rust on the beans was reduced but angular leaf spot increased. Cowpea viruses were reduced when cowpeas were combined with cassava or plantain. In these mixtures, and in a cowpea-maize combination, the severity of Asochyta leafspot and powdery mildew on the cowpeas was also reduced.[120] Other disease-resisting crop combinations include maize-sunflowers-oats-sesame, potato-mustards, and okra-tomato-ginger-mungbean under coconut trees. Viruses, fungi, and nematodes are all affected by selected mixtures of plants. Just how the diseases are reduced is not always known, but some cases indicate that chemicals produced by one plant may help another ward off attack. Also, the plant community's physical structure may inhibit liberation, dissemination, and reproduction of disease-causing agents.[121]

In some polycultures, insects may also be less damaging. Multiple cropping simply spreads the risk of loss among several crops instead of wagering all on a single one. Beyond that, however, several factors in the spatial and temporal arrangement of plants can influence insect population dynamics.[122] Mixed-crop stands may affect the visual or olfactory stimuli that help insects find food. Several studies of aphids and other pests have shown that some species are drawn to areas where plants stand out against bare soil; they are less interested in solid green backgrounds resulting from dense intercrops. Insects that feed only on particular food plants may miss their targets if the crop is mixed with other, equally aromatic, plants. For instance, in experiments, cabbage-feeding beetles found it hard to colonize plants and reproduce where tomato and tobacco were interplanted with collards. As a result, leaf damage fell by 75 percent compared to pure stands. Laboratory experiments confirmed that odors from tomato and tobacco inhibited the insect from feeding and remaining on its host plant.[123]

In some mixtures, insects can be drawn to one crop instead of another that is more vulnerable to damage. Cowpeas, for instance, appear to be protected from insect attack by interplanting with such cereals as sorghum, and okra seems to divert flea beetles from cotton, a more valuable crop.[124] The ability of insects to disperse through a field can also be impeded if crops of differing size and structure are mixed. Damage by another cowpea pest was cut when maize was planted in the same rows as the cowpeas. Sometimes, one crop can be planted in barrier strips or "guard rows" around another. Planting soybeans around pigeon peas, for example, prevents the immigration of hairy caterpillars.[125] Planting mixtures can also improve habitat for insects' natural enemies, especially such general predators as spiders and ground beetles. Specialists, such as many species of parasitic wasps, may be inhibited if they are as confused by visual or olfactory stimuli in mixtures as their prey are.

Overall, insect pests seem more often reduced than encouraged by mixtures. In a review of about 150 studies of plant-feeding insects, researchers found that over 60 percent of the populations and over 50 percent of the species observed were less abundant in mixtures than in monocultures. In contrast, only about 11 percent of populations and 18 percent of species increased in mixtures.[126] According to a related review of the likely mechanisms that favor mixtures as a way of managing pests, most studies attributed polyculture's success primarily to the difficulty that insects encounter trying to find enough of their

Multiple cropping simply spreads the risk of loss among several crops instead of wagering all on a single one.

preferred food plants to survive and reproduce, not to the influence of natural enemies on pest populations.[127]

Weed control can also be enhanced in multiple-cropping systems. When intercropped with cucurbits in the Congo basin, with sweet potatoes or mungbeans in the Philippines, and with beans in Colombia, maize has to compete with fewer weeds because light-demanding weeds are shaded out. A cassava-bean combination in Colombia produced the same effect. Other intercrops, such as cowpea-sorghum-millet in Nigeria and maize-rice-cassava in Indonesia, achieved similar results through somewhat different mechanisms.[128] Commonly in polycultures, the combined vegetation of the various crops leaves little room for weeds to invade or survive, and the efficiency with which crop mixtures use light, water, and nutrients reduces opportunities for weed competition. A wide array of plant species, both crops and weeds, have been found to produce and disseminate—by volatilization from leaves or exudation from roots—chemicals that inhibit the growth or survival of nearby plants. Crop plants with these "allelopathic" properties could be contributing to weed control in mixed plantings, and the possibility of breeding such traits into crops is being explored.[129]

Weeds and weeding often severely hamper agricultural production. But some "weeds" may in fact be resources. Traditional farmers surveyed in Mexico held highly sophisticated views of noncrop plants as beneficial at certain times and densities, and detrimental at others. To these farmers, "clean cultivation," a goal in many technologically advanced cropping systems, is a distinct disadvantage.[130] And a survey of noncrop plants in Indian ricefields found dozens of species with potential practical value as medicinal, industrial, and food products.[131] A broad view of the role of all plants in an agroecosystem—and how to favor those combinations best suited to meeting human needs—could spare agriculture the expenses and environmental consequences of excessive weed control.

At one time, the advantages of polyculture might simply have been attributed to the "stabilizing role of species diversity."[132] But a more sound explanation of diversity's role will benefit not only ecology but the development of polyculture as an agroecosystem-design strategy. Underlying the new view of diversity in agriculture is the critical distinction between *natural* diversity and *planned* diversity. Diversity in an agroecosystem cannot be increased randomly, any more than an engineer randomly designs redundant features into, say, a bridge or spacecraft. Just as the engineer carefully chooses which elements to back up with substitute or alternative capabilities, so too the farmer or the scientist selects specific species, spatial and temporal arrangements, and management tactics to repond to different needs, including that of ecosystem stability. Much of the diversity found in indigenous agroecosystems undoubtedly arose not so much from an ecological understanding as from economic or subsistence need. A sufficiently wide array of crops means that something is always being harvested, so there is always something to eat or sell. Crop diversity

Underlying the new view of diversity in agriculture is the critical distinction between **natural** *diversity and* **planned** *diversity.*

also provides a hedge against unexpected weather changes: if one crop fails because of too much or too little rain, another crop may survive or even thrive. Mixed-crop systems meet more of the cash- and credit-poor subsistence farming family's annual needs with less risk than monocropping. And multiple cropping tends to spread labor demand throughout the growing season rather than in peaks.[133]

With economic concerns or subsistence stability in mind, traditional farmers have selected systems with diversity in species composition, plant structures (both above and below ground), plant chemistry (such as allelopathic properties and defenses against pests), and plant nutrition (such as water and nutrient requirements). Complex above-ground plant architecture allows these evolved agroecosystems to maximize the use of light. Because the root structures of the various species are layered, these systems also make good use of available water and minerals. Deep-rooted plants can act as "nutrient pumps," bringing up minerals from deep soil layers to counteract leaching. The soil structure stays stable or improves as organic matter is added to the soil year after year, as suggested in the Mexican maize-bean intercrop. Mulches, more complete ground cover, and dense crop canopies can keep weed problems in check, and appropriate combinations of crops and cropping practices can reduce damage from insects and diseases. Where legumes are part of the polyculture, soil nitrogen (often a constraint on increasing productivity) can be conserved, even increased.[134]

Scientists generally agree that indigenous multiple-cropping systems are not as productive as they could be. Some high-yielding varieties (HYVs) bred for use in more input-intensive cropping programs fare well in mixed-crop environments as well, especially the less competitive varieties. Other desirable characteristics for intercropped HYVs include photoperiod insensitivity (independence of daylength for growth and development), early maturity, resistance to insects and diseases, and population responsiveness (which allows farmers to vary plant densities in accordance with the particular needs of mixtures). Most important, new varieties have to be tested in typical mixtures and environments.[135]

As important as new plant varieties are to agricultural development, they represent but one dimension in the picture. In an agroecosystem, wide-ranging physical and biological factors shape plants' and animals' growth patterns, population densities, productivity, and stability. Many of these factors are manipulable. The choice of species in a mixture, the spacing among plants, the timing of planting and harvesting, the amount and timing of fertilizer applications, the control of the water supply, and the application of pest-control measures can all be used to enhance productivity, sustainability, or both. In this context, plant breeding becomes one of many tools at the disposal of the agroecosystem designer, rather than an end in itself: the system design dictates the selection of plant characters for breeding instead of the other way around.

A Modified Polycultural Agroecosystem in Mexico

In the state of Tabasco, Mexico, traditional subsistence agriculture was largely abandoned in favor of commercial farming and stock-raising in the 1960s and 1970s. Not only was locally grown food less available, but expected productivity increases failed to materialize. The area's agriculture has shifted to export crops and cattle, while large areas of once-productive land have been deserted as intensive cultivation or overgrazing wore out the thin tropical soils. To help reclaim these areas, researchers have designed and installed production units based in part on indigenous polyculture and in part on the application of ecological knowledge.[136]

In the Tabascan project, each production unit consists of a forest shelter belt, a water-storage tank or reservoir, raised-earth areas for vegetable production, and areas for growing staple annual crops and fruits. *(See Figure 3.)* In the reservoirs, fish and ducks are raised. Reservoir sediments and aquatic plants are used as fertilizer for crops and to construct "chinampas"—raised beds whose design dates back to the ancient Mayan civilization.[137] Organic matter from the reservoirs and manure from pigs, chickens, and ducks (fed on excess or spoiled produce) enrich the soil of the chinampas continually. This strategy for maintaining soil fertility resembles that employed in many Javanese home-gardens, where ponds are built for the multiple purposes of processing human and animal waste, raising fish, and returning sediment to the soil.[138]

On the chinampas, traditional mixtures of crops, primarily vegetables, are cultivated intensively. Tomatoes, chilies, onions, melons, and other annuals predominate, though such perennials as papaya, plantain, and cassava may also be grown. Among basic annuals, the maize-bean-squash combination is usually preferred, with a scattering of perennials. Some rice is also cultivated. Fruit and bean trees—including cacao, guanabana, mango, coffee, citrus, and coconut—as well as pineapples, populate areas of perennial production. With this broad array of species, some food is always available for harvest, every usable patch of ground is covered by plants, and light is more completely utilized. High biomass accumulation is a necessity of this system, and the high crop diversity contributes more biomass than monocrop systems while also providing additional harvestable food. Legume cover crops in the annual crops areas provide sufficient organic matter and nitrogen to maintain soil fertility and may also help control weeds, nematodes, and diseases.

Pest management in these production units requires no commercial chemical pesticides. The forest shelter belts probably act as reserves for numerous predators and parasites of insect pests, and the high structural and species diversity of the cropping systems also favors these beneficial organisms. Relying on local plant varieties for all crops, scientists also believe, enables the systems to make the most of resistance to insects and diseases that has already evolved in the area's traditional agriculture. The crop mixtures, cover crops, and rota-

Figure 3. Diagrammatic Representations of the Production Units in Tabasco, Mexico.

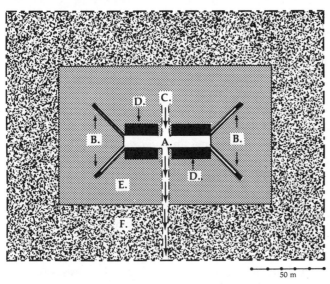

1. Where the lowest part of the unit can be centrally located, large tanks (A) are constructed as catchments for runoff to collect nutrients and soil, sometimes with the aid of runoff canals (B). A drainage canal (C) prevents inundation of the site. Other features are raised-earth vegetable-production areas known as "chinampas" (D), areas of annual and perennial cropping (E), and a forest shelter belt (F).

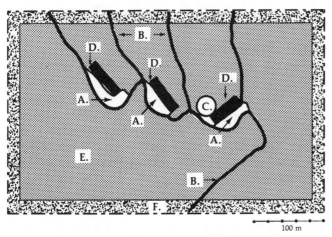

2. Where topographic conditions allow, reservoirs (A) and natural water courses (B) are used instead of tanks and canals. A duck pen (C) is also shown in this diagram. Chinampas (D), annual/perennial cropping areas (E), and a forest shelter belt (F) are basic to the system design.

Source: Stephen R. Gliessman, *et al.,* "The Ecological Basis for the Application of Traditional Agricultural Technology in the Management of Tropical Agro-Ecosystems," *Agro-Ecosystems* 7 (1981): 173-85.

tions used in the production units also appear to control weeds adequately.

Although the systems currently use only indigenous species and varieties, there is room for improvement. New species, such as winged bean, may be introduced in the future, though they will not replace native crops. Similarly, cassava breeders in South America encourage farmers to add new varieties to their usual mixtures but not to abandon the old. This approach ensures a continuing supply of genetic diversity for future breeding and—more important—preserves the farmer's options should the new varieties fail to cope with environmental or other changes.[139]

The Tabasco project applies several key ecological principles to agriculture. First, wherever possible, the systems employ traditional crops, crop mixtures, and management practices. Most innovation has been in agroecosystem architecture, with the introduction of the chinampas, reservoirs, and forest shelter belts. Second, the project emphasizes the accumulation of the organic matter needed to improve soil structure and fertility through the combined use of reservoir sediments, animal manures, and crop residues. Third, a cornerstone of the overall design of the agroecosystem is diversity—crop diversity in the mixtures, structural diversity in plant architecture, and species diversity in the crop/forest/reservoir system. This diversity offers security in harvestable food and appears to help protect crops from pests. Finally, the Tabasco project is especially attuned to local ecological and topographical conditions. In short, it shows that ecological principles and practical knowledge can be successfully combined to create self-renewing agricultural production systems.

Agroforestry: Farming with Trees

Aboriginal farming systems have probably always included trees. Although the swidden agricultural cycle is usually described as clearing a field from forest, then abandoning it when the soil loses its fertility, the demarcations are not quite so clear. Shifting cultivators often spare trees of value for fruit or fodder. And clearings are rarely abandoned abruptly. As trees regrow, farmers may sow some crops among them or harvest perennials planted at the beginning of the cycle. Some swidden farmers plant seedlings of valued tree species that will mature during the "fallow" period, providing additional food, fodder, and firewood for years after annual cropping has ceased. Indeed, the Javanese home-garden has been described as a human-directed successional system, wherein the evolution from cleared-field rice production to multi-storied garden is carefully controlled through planting and selective removal of plants over several years.[140]

In the last decade, scientists and development specialists have become increasingly interested in the merger of crop, animal, and tree production commonly called agroforestry. Spurred by deforestation, soil erosion, and the ever-growing need for both fuelwood and sustainable upland food production, agroforestry advocates have been

Ecological principles and practical knowledge can be successfully combined to create self-renewing agricultural production systems.

exploring a wide variety of crop-tree, animal-tree, and crop-animal-tree combinations in both indigenous and newly designed farming systems.[141] Shifting agriculture is the oldest form of traditional agroforestry, while planted fallows is a common form of improved swidden.[142] In the late 19th century, the British introduced a reforestation technique known as "Taungya," in which food is produced among newly planted trees, and discontinued when the forest canopy grows dense enough to preclude continued cropping. Perhaps the best system for improving agriculture is simultaneous and continuous tree and food cropping, or "integral agroforestry."[143]

Trees play many roles in agroforestry. Besides providing such useful products as fuelwood, poles, fruit, edible seeds or beans, and fodder, they also minimize nutrient drain due to leaching and soil erosion, restore nutrients lost from the ecosystem, and perform other key environmental services.[144] Planted as "living fences," trees can keep grazing animals out of crop areas. They serve as windbreaks or as shade trees in pastures and fields, helping to improve the microclimate so that animals and plants have better chances of survival.[145] Trees with long tap roots for anchorage and wide-spreading lateral roots bind the soil and prevent erosion. These tap roots draw mineral nutrients up from the lower soil strata. Nitrogen-fixing trees also produce nitrates that can be recycled from decomposed leaves into the cropping system along with the "pumped" nutrients. Of course, the trees used in agroforestry must perform these functions without harming or competing with the understory vegetation, and should have relatively thin crowns to allow as much sunlight as possible to reach the plants nearer the ground. *(See Figure 4.)* Ideal for many combined crop-tree agroforestry systems are such leguminous trees as *Leucaena*, *Acacia*, and *Gliricidia*.[146] In situations where nitrogen-fixation is less important, fruit trees or coffee, cacao, or coconut trees may fit local ecological and economic needs better.

Agroforestry may be particularly important in revitalizing upland agriculture. Often, increased population pressure and land hunger have led people to intensify agriculture on hilly lands (often misapplying lowland farming methods) only to cause rapid deforestation, soil erosion, and loss of productivity. Many of these lands have degenerated into virtually unusable grasslands. Although terracing reduces erosion and helps conserve water, it is back-breaking, time-consuming work. If erosion is proceeding rapidly, the time and labor needed to prevent large soil losses may not be available. Agroforestry offers an economical alternative. In one scheme, trees are planted in strips of two or more rows across the slope, alternating with strips of such food crops as maize. If trees are planted densely enough, the strips become soil fences, trapping soil coming downhill. *(See Figure 5.)* With fast-growing trees, terraces can be established in as little as three years, though close spacing precludes production of much fuelwood or timber and trees must be pruned regularly so that crops are not overshaded.[147]

In most cases, agroforestry serves many objectives. If legume trees

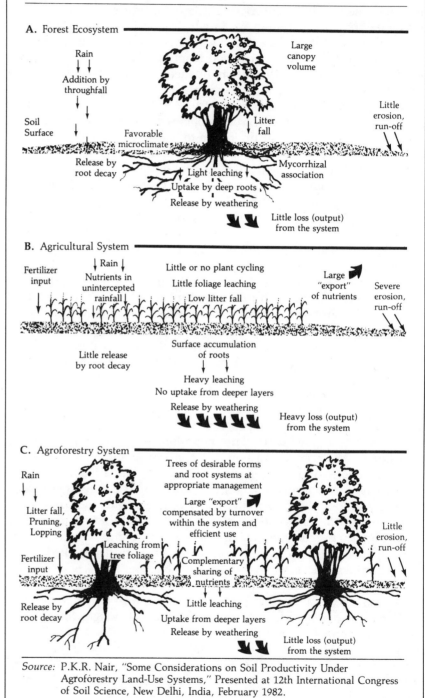

Figure 4. Schematic Representation of Nutrient Relations and Advantages of Agroforestry Systems (C) in Comparison with Forestry (A) and Agricultural (B) Systems.

A. Forest Ecosystem

Rain

Addition by throughfall

Soil Surface

Favorable microclimate

Litter fall

Large canopy volume

Little erosion, run-off

Release by root decay

Light leaching

Mycorrhizal association

Uptake by deep roots

Release by weathering

Little loss (output) from the system

B. Agricultural System

Fertilizer input

Rain

Nutrients in unintercepted rainfall

Little or no plant cycling

Little foliage leaching

Low litter fall

Large "export" of nutrients

Severe erosion, run-off

Little release by root decay

Surface accumulation of roots

Heavy leaching

No uptake from deeper layers

Release by weathering

Heavy loss (output) from the system

C. Agroforestry System

Rain

Litter fall, Pruning, Lopping

Fertilizer input

Trees of desirable forms and root systems at appropriate management

Large "export" compensated by turnover within the system and efficient use

Leaching from tree foliage

Complementary sharing of nutrients

Little erosion, run-off

Release by root decay

Little leaching

Uptake from deeper layers

Release by weathering

Little loss (output) from the system

Source: P.K.R. Nair, "Some Considerations on Soil Productivity Under Agroforestry Land-Use Systems," Presented at 12th International Congress of Soil Science, New Delhi, India, February 1982.

Figure 5. Strip Cropping with Trees to Form Natural Terraces

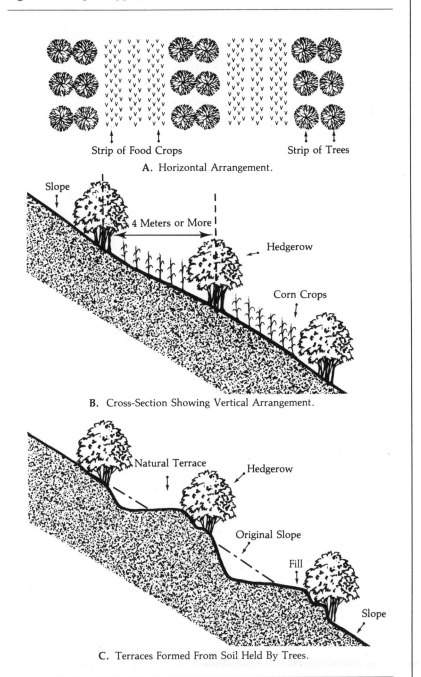

Strip of Food Crops   Strip of Trees

A. Horizontal Arrangement.

Slope

4 Meters or More

Hedgerow

Corn Crops

B. Cross-Section Showing Vertical Arrangement.

Natural Terrace   Hedgerow

Original Slope

Fill

Slope

C. Terraces Formed From Soil Held By Trees.

Source: Napoleon T. Vergara, ed., *New Directions in Agroforestry: The Potential of Tropical Legume Trees* (Honolulu, Hawaii: Environment and Policy Institute, East-West Center, 1982).

are used, their leaves and branches can be mulched to provide nitrogen to growing crops. In trials at the International Institute of Tropical Agriculture in Nigeria, *Leucaena* tops added to the soil contributed over 200 kilograms of nitrogen per hectare in two years, giving yields of over 2,800 kilograms of maize per hectare (considered "acceptable" by Institute researchers). The trees and maize were "alley cropped," (planted in alternating strips) which allows fertilizing and weeding in the crop rows while retaining the benefits of intercropping. Also, the trees grew so rapidly that weed growth was suppressed, erosion prevented, and (in a planted swidden fallow) soil fertility restored quickly.[148]

In semi-arid Africa, trees can help restore the land to productive use. The indigenous *Acacia albida,* a legume, is a valuable component of a mixed-farming system that also includes millet, sorghum, and cattle. Where *Acacia* was left in Sudanese fields, millet could be grown continuously for 15 to 20 years, compared to only 3 to 5 years without the tree. In Senegal, one researcher found that, when the crop-livestock-tree system was kept in balance, the land could support 50 to 60 people per hectare (several times the average for the region) with continuous cropping and no loss of soil productivity. *Acacia albida* drops its leaves during the rainy season when crops are grown, thus releasing nitrogen and organic matter into the soil, and allowing light to reach the crops. As a result, soil quality is improved and crop yields are greatly enhanced. *(See Table 8.)* In the dry season, the tree produces leaves and pods, providing fodder and shade for cattle whose dung further improves the soil.[149]

Integrating trees with farming has been a key element in the African assistance program jointly sponsored by CARE and the U.S. Agency for International Development. In Chad, CARE helped establish *Acacia* on over 6,000 hectares of farmers' fields. In spite of civil war and unfavorable weather, up to 80 percent of the trees planted between 1975 and 1978 survived through 1985. Other tree species were used to create living hedges and woodlots, protecting gardens and cropland from grazing animals and providing villagers with much-needed shade, poles, and fuel.[150] CARE also helped farmers in the Majjia Valley combat desertification due to topsoil erosion by establishing windbreaks of neem trees. Another benefit is that, in the areas protected by windbreaks, grain yield per kilogram of water used is over 40 percent higher than in open areas. Most farmers in the program reported increased crop yields, and total dry matter production went up by about 33 percent in protected areas.[151]

Agroforestry plays a major part in a development and reclamation project at Nyabisindu, Rwanda, where intense shifting cultivation, fuelwood exploitation, and overgrazing have rapidly eroded soil on completely denuded hillsides. Attempts to introduce Western-style agriculture to the region have failed, partly because the required inputs are so expensive but more because supplies are so frequently interrupted. To help solve these farmers' problems, researchers turned to methods based on local skills and resources and oriented toward

Table 8. Effects of *Acacia albida* trees on soil characteristics and crop yields in Africa

A. Nutrients returned annually to the topsoil

Element	Amount (kg./ha.)
Nitrogen	186
Phosphorus	4
Potassium	76
Calcium	222
Magnesium	39

B. Increases in soil quality and yield under *Acacia* crowns

Item	Percent increase
Total soil nitrogen	33–110
Organic matter	40–269
Cation exchange capacity	50–120
Millet yields	37–104
Sorghum yield	105

Source: Michael McGuahey, ''Impact of Forestry Initiatives in the Sahel'' (Washington, D.C.: Chemonics International, 1986).

recycling of nutrients. Many traditional Rwandese farmers already practiced mulching and some raised-field agriculture, while farmers in the neighboring East African highlands had developed a self-sustaining agriculture that supported a large population on similarly thin soils by incorporating multi-storied intercropping of trees and crops, stall-feeding livestock with fodder crops, use of organic fertilizers (animal manure, composting, and ''green manure''), high diversity of crops, and erosion control through contour planting and mulching.

At Nyabisindu, a complex system combining trees, animals, and crops was developed, building on the community's existing knowledge and applying ecological criteria in the development of new methods. Trees and hedges were used to establish erosion-control strips yielding fruit, wood, and fodder, protecting the soil, and improving microclimates. Woodlots with pine, eucalyptus, *Leucaena*, and other species were planted at higher elevations where farming was not possible. In the cropping areas, extensive use was made of perennial crops to further stabilize the soil. Highly diverse crop mixtures were planted, both to take advantage of the ecological characteristics of polycultures and to reduce risk of loss from pests, weather, or market vagaries. Organic fertilizing with animal manure, mulches, and compost served to recycle wastes, raise the soil's humus content, and reduce leaching and soil-borne pest problems. Stabled animals were fed on fodder crops and leaves from hedges and erosion-control strips. And where mineral fertilizers were necessary, local sources of rock with the needed elements were sought out and used.

A key to the project's success is a tree nursery that produces about five million trees annually. Fruit trees on farmland, shade trees along roadsides, and small forests on hilltops are all part of reforestation in the region. Intercropped with the trees on the farms are combinations of such cash crops as bananas, coffee, and avocadoes, and such subsistence species as beans, maize, cassava, soybeans, and sweet potatoes. Fodder including grasses, sorghum, and legumes supplies food to livestock. (See Figure 6.) Results from test plots indicate that a typical farm family using the mixed crop-tree system could produce 25 to 50 percent more fuelwood than it needs. Experimental data also showed that three-crop mixtures in the system provided 54 percent more calories, 31 percent more protein, and 62 percent more carbohydrates than do monocultures.[152]

At Nyabisindu, stabled livestock are an important part of the agro-ecosystem, providing manure for fertilization and meat for better nutrition. A regeneration strategy for upland areas in the Philippines likewise uses caged goats as part of a production system including a forage legume, native grasses, and Leucaena and Gliricidia trees.[153] In other areas, agroforestry integrates trees with permanent pasture and grazing animals. In West Africa, local breeds of dwarf sheep and goats could become an important source of protein if an adequate feed supply can be maintained and problems with disease overcome. Properly managed, pasture may be the best use for marginal lands that cannot support cropping, and planting leguminous trees on them can enhance productivity. Belts of trees placed between pastures can provide shade, food for livestock, and timber for construction and firewood, at the same time shielding the animals and the pasture ecosystem from wind, cold, and water stress. Livestock can also eat fodder from legume trees growing in strip- or alley-cropping arrangements with food plants.[154]

In Amazonian Ecuador, tropical forest sheep are used to intensify production on swidden fallows. Shifting cultivators are encouraged to plant contour strips of Inga edulis, a deep-rooted leguminous fuelwood tree, along with cassava. After the cassava is harvested, a perennial leguminous ground cover, Desmodium, is planted between the trees. This easily established and vigorous ground cover cascades over banks and steep slopes to help bind soil and control erosion. Also, the grazing sheep find Desmodium reasonably palatable, and the animals return fecal matter to the soil, stimulating the symbiosis between the legumes and their associated nitrogen-fixing bacteria. Unlike cattle, these sheep cause little soil compaction and erosion, and sheep can produce three times as much meat per hectare as cattle. The tree-groundcover-sheep combination thus provides fuelwood and meat protein to farmers while preserving and improving the soil during the fallow.[155]

Figure 6. Example of Model Farm in Nyabisindu, Rwanda.

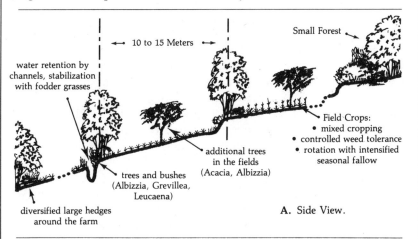

10 to 15 Meters

water retention by channels, stabilization with fodder grasses

Small Forest

additional trees in the fields (Acacia, Albizzia)

Field Crops:
• mixed cropping
• controlled weed tolerance
• rotation with intensified seasonal fallow

trees and bushes (Albizzia, Grevillea, Leucaena)

diversified large hedges around the farm

A. Side View.

B. Typical Horizontal Layout of Model Farm, ± 1 Hectare

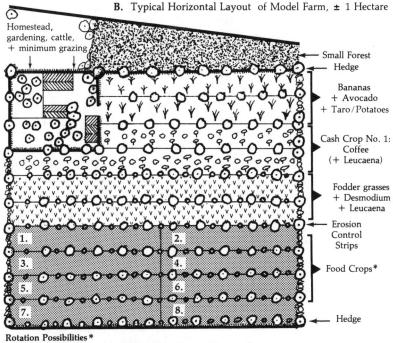

Homestead, gardening, cattle, + minimum grazing

Small Forest

Hedge

Bananas
+ Avocado
+ Taro / Potatoes

Cash Crop No. 1:
Coffee
(+ Leucaena)

Fodder grasses
+ Desmodium
+ Leucaena

Erosion
Control
Strips

Food Crops*

Hedge

Rotation Possibilities*
1. Feb.: Mucuna Fallow & Sunflower; Oct.: Beans & Maize
2. Feb.: Soja & Sorghum; Oct.: Soja & Maize
3. Feb.: Cassava & Mucuna 4° Season; Oct.: Cassava & Mucuna 2° Season
4. Feb.: Cassava & Mucuna 4° Season; Oct.: Cassava & M. 4°s, Harvest
5. Feb.: Soja & Sorghum; Oct.: Soja & Maize
6. Feb.: Mucuna Fallow & Sunflower; Oct.: Beans & Maize
7. Feb.: Sweet Potatoes & Soja; Oct.: Soja & Maize
8. Feb.: Soja & Maize; Oct.: Beans & Maize

Source: Friedrich Behmel and Irmfried Neumann, "An Example for Agro-Forestry in Tropical Mountain Areas," Presented to the workshop on *Agro-Forestry in The African Humid Tropics*, Ibadan, Nigeria, 1981.

RASMUSON LIBRARY
UNIVERSITY OF ALASKA-FAIRBANKS

Agroforestry as a modern applied science is still in an early stage of development. Basic principles are reasonably well worked out, but few case studies have had the longevity needed for in-depth analysis. As the Nyabisindu project demonstrates, mixing trees and crops is not always appropriate, especially at higher elevations there. In some lowlands, permanent agriculture with little if any integration with trees may be feasible and, given production needs, preferable, though agroforestry may be important in the transition from shifting to permanent agriculture[156] and in the restoration of degraded lands. Agroforestry is also running the risk of becoming too closely identified with large-scale plantings of tree species not native to a developing area. In fact, very few native species have been adequately studied for use in agroforestry programs, though such indigenous trees may prove best suited to local needs. In the Sahel, for example, the locally adapted *Acacia* grows better than such imported species as eucalyptus planted on similar sites.[157] As promising as *Leucaena* appears to be, it is not suited to all soils, cropping systems, or climates, and recent experiments demonstrate that *Leucaena* leaves are toxic to rice plants.[158] Certainly, great care must be taken to select trees that fit local conditions and to preserve tree species diversity. Despite such possible limitations, however, agroforestry's potential for meeting a multiplicity of economic and ecological needs in agricultural development has clearly been demonstrated.

Emerging Agroecological Principles

The foremost rule of agroecology is that there is no substitute for detailed knowledge of the specific site being developed or managed. Principles, theories, even apparent ''laws,'' must bend to the reality of what is actually happening. What ecology offers agriculture is not a set of easy answers but rather a set of difficult questions.

In any ecological analysis of an agricultural system, understanding the performance of the system as a whole is as important as examining the structure and dynamics of the parts. In one approach to interdisciplinary agroecosystem analysis developed by Gordon Conway of Imperial College in London, four essential system properties have been identified: productivity (level of output), stability (constancy or persistence of output over time), sustainability (ability to recover from stress and perturbations), and equitability (evenness of the distribution of benefits among income groups or social classes).[159] Experience in conducting workshops for research planning, principally in Asia, has shown that these properties encompass many of the important elements of agroecosystem structure and function at a regional level, though they are not all-inclusive. According to anthropologist A. Terry Rambo of the East-West Center in Hawaii, dependence on, or autonomy from, other ecosystems may be a key factor in understanding an agroecosystem. Lowland agriculture in many areas of the world, for instance, often depends heavily on the washing of nutrients from uplands for its fertility. Thus, one ecosystem may be able to maintain

What ecology offers agriculture is not a set of easy answers but rather a set of difficult questions.

50

its productivity only as another degrades.[160] Such dependence can also undermine both systems, as when uplands degrade so far that they can no longer retain water or soil, and lowland areas suffer flooding and silting of irrigation systems as a result.[161] In Rambo's terminology, the converse of dependency is compatibility: the effects of an agroecosystem on other biological or social systems. If, for example, chemicals from a pest-control program contaminate drinking water, the agroecosystem using those chemicals is incompatible with the health system of the people supposedly benefiting from effective pest control.

Another property of agroecosystems that may be of considerable importance is energy efficiency.[162] Where energy is derived from fossil fuel, direct monetary costs and benefits of system designs' efficiency can be calculated. If labor or animal power is chiefly used instead, the costs and benefits of efficiency may be expressed more in terms of alternative uses of the person's or animal's time. Still, judging a production system solely on the basis of energy efficiency would be a mistake. Farmers seek to optimize several, often competing, aspects of their operation, and energy efficiency (producing more calories per calorie expended) may be less important than producing enough protein. Although less solar energy is captured by people when they eat meat than when they consume plants directly, some marginal lands may best supply human needs through well-managed livestock and forage production rather than planting food crops.

A key objective regarding energy efficiency in agriculture should be to find ways to substitute structure for energy in the maintenance of the ecosystem. Multi-storied plant canopies can capture greater amounts of sunlight, which in turn can produce larger amounts of biomass that would otherwise need such energy-intensive inputs as fertilizers. And adding animals to the farm system can mean that more plant material is turned into usable food. This may be the real value of the high diversity that characterizes so much agroecological experimentation, though diversity also distributes both ecological and economic risk so that growth of one crop can sometimes compensate for losses of another.

Economic and ecological considerations often converge in strategies to develop sustainable agriculture. Consider the use of fertilizers. Agriculture is highly dependent on proper timing of management practices. In landlocked Rwanda, for example, political unrest in neighboring countries can interrupt supplies of commercial fertilizers and pesticides.[163] The world over, poor road conditions, lack of vehicles, and diversion of chemicals to the black market can also disrupt supplies of critical agricultural inputs. Then too, as the Administrator of the U.S. Agency for International Development recently remarked, it costs more to transport fertilizer from an African port to the interior of the country, where it is needed, than it does to ship the material from the United States to Africa.[164] In Rwanda, a ton of fertilizer that sells on the world market for $200 can cost $600 after transport costs from the port at Mombasa, Kenya, are added on.[165] If those inputs are not available when the soil or the crops need them, the entire crop can be lost. Ecological considerations alone would favor making maximal use of biological sources of nutrients and pest control, but the cost and uncertainty of supply of external inputs give the biological alternative an economic basis as well. Similarly, increased diversity in the agroecosystem may serve ecological functions of increasing biomass productivity and risk-spreading, *and* also improve diets by providing a wider array of vitamins and minerals, *and* give farmers more products to sell at different times of year.

Applying ecological principles to agriculture raises several policy issues. Chiefly, what is the best way to implement sustainable agricultural systems? And what are the consequences of implementing them? Successful programs are grounded in indigenous farming practices, farmers' active involvement in decision-making on research and implementation, an emphasis on local resources instead of external inputs, and a strong stake on farmers' part in the program's outcome. If sustainable agriculture is to become a reality, policy decisions will have to be made on such issues as land tenure and land use, market structure, subsidies, research and extension structures and priorities, local political autonomy, and distribution and pricing of food. How policy-makers address these and similar concerns will largely determine whether sustainable agricultural systems can be designed and put into use.

V. Policy Issues Raised by an Ecological Approach

The State of Knowledge: Definitions, Assumptions, and Experts

Future historians of agriculture may well come to look upon the last half of the twentieth century as a curious developmental detour, characterized by sizable energy subsidies, resource-depleting practices, and a constricted research focus. Much has been learned today about increasing productivity by applying industrially based inputs, but wide gaps in our understanding of the fundamental processes underlying agriculture remain. And practical applications of the ecological approach are small and scattered, with little quantitative evidence accumulating to support wider adoption. Clearly, a substantial research program is needed to put ecological technologies on an equal footing with the well-researched industrial technologies. In addition, other constraints will have to be addressed if agriculture is to become ecologically sustainable.

The future of agricultural development will depend in large part on what "experts" say and do about it. Conflict and controversy continue in the agricultural science community over the future of agriculture. What one person or organization may consider useful research on sustainable agriculture might be labeled wrong-headed or irrelevant by others. Use of *any* agricultural chemicals may be rejected by some as unsustainable, while others may refuse to believe that biologically based farming practices can ever meet food needs. Assistance organizations and development ministries often call on scientists to help them decide what projects to fund or how to judge the performance of those projects. But few if any scientists are free of biases inherent in their training, experience, and peer relationships.

For many reasons, there has been remarkably little ecological research on traditional farming systems and very little applied research and development on the application of ecological principles to agricultural development. For the past half century, virtually the entire focus of agriculture in industrialized countries has been on increasingly energy-intensive and high-input, but labor-efficient and high-yielding farming methods. This approach has produced dramatic increases in Western agricultural productivity, along with the dogma,

Future historians of agriculture may well come to look upon the last half of the twentieth century as a curious developmental detour, characterized by sizable energy subsidies, resource-depleting practices, and a constricted research focus.

53

doctrine, and experience of virtually all of today's agricultural specialists. Through the technical assistance process, the experience of industrial nations has been disseminated throughout much of the developing world.

The orientation of agricultural education is probably the most important single constraint to the broader development and application of ecologically sustainable agriculture. Agricultural educational institutions focussing on labor-efficient, high-input, high-yield-per-unit-area, industrial-type agriculture produce the agricultural scientists, development advisors, and other experts for the developed world. The agricultural staff and advisors of development assistance agencies come from the same pool, as do many of the agricultural experts and government officials from the Third World.

On the other side of the coin, the term "sustainable agriculture" has, at least in the United States, been appropriated to some extent by advocates of such alternative agricultural methods as organic farming. Since these people coined the term and first raised the issue of sustainability, they have every right to "authorship." But, unfortunately, the close association with organic farming, legitimate as it may be, can also make farmers and scientists oriented toward more "conventional"—that is, chemical-intensive—agriculture needlessly critical. To some extent, supporters of the concept of sustainable agriculture are considered outside the traditional agricultural research/extension system in the developed countries, and they see themselves as pitted against the agricultural establishment. In fact, organic farming has gotten short shrift from the U.S. Land Grant system and the U.S. Department of Agriculture, though both do support a little research into alternative agricultural methods.

In fact, no single agricultural method has a corner on sustainability. Any farming system, whether chemical-intensive or "natural," can be resource-conserving or wasteful, environmentally sound or polluting. Obviously, serious questions surround how long such external energy and nutrient subsidies as fossil fuels, petrochemicals, and mined mineral fertilizers can be maintained. But simply substituting non-chemical alternatives may not necessarily make agriculture more sustainable. For example, a nonchemical weed-control program, unless managed carefully, can be more energy-intensive and cause more soil erosion than a herbicide-based program. And applying animal manures unwisely can pollute ground and surface waters as badly as overuse of chemical fertilizers can.

By the same token, productivity is not the sole province of industrial agriculture. Productivity is most commonly thought of as crop yield per hectare, and one easy way to increase yields is to apply chemical fertilizers. Polyculture, too, can often provide better yields than monoculture, as we have shown. But productivity can also be measured as yield per unit of labor, energy, cash, or purchased inputs. Often, farmers improve their cropping system according to one measure at the "expense" of another. Defining farm systems' success strictly in terms of yield per unit area (and concluding that ecological agriculture

Defining farm systems' success strictly in terms of yield per unit area (and concluding that ecological agriculture is relatively unproductive) misses agroecologists' point that yield, stability, environmental quality, and net income to the farmer must all be optimized.

is relatively unproductive) misses agroecologists' point that yield, stability, environmental quality, and net income to the farmer must all be optimized.

The apparent conflict between the "stewardship" and "food-sufficiency" schools of thought needs to give way to a multi-dimensional view of agroecosystem performance. Where the measure of performance is limited to short-term increases in crop output, relying heavily on purchased inputs may well seem superior to less chemical-intensive alternatives. But if net economic gain is also a goal, something considerably less than maximum levels of purchased inputs may be preferable. And if environmental quality is a concern, still fewer chemicals may be acceptable. Most likely, as energy and chemical inputs are reduced to meet economic or environmental requirements, the "information content" of agroecosystems—expressed as species diversity, complex crop architecture, or sophisticated management strategies—will increase.

Criticisms that biologically based agricultural methods are not productive enough need to be seen in this context. In the face of ever-increasing human populations and hunger, increased yield has long been a major objective of many development-assistance programs, and farmers' net economic benefit and longer-term ecological sustainability has at best been secondary. But where production gains have been realized, economics and sustainability are now becoming important. And where productivity increases have failed to occur, or where agricultural "improvements" have wrought environmental disaster, the linkages between economics and ecology are becoming more apparent.

China provides a good example. In the 1970s, recognizing the need to increase production to feed a quarter of the world's population, the government embarked on a high-input agricultural program. It imported chemical fertilizers and pesticides, and it developed and greatly expanded China's own industrial capacity to produce these chemicals. In six years, the Chinese tripled the use of chemical fertilizers, and production of fertilized crops increased by 50 percent.[166]

Yet chemicals were not necessarily the heroes in this story. At the same time that use of fertilizers and pesticides was being increased, the shift from fully communal agriculture to private enterprise was taking place, so farmers had incentives to increase production. And now questions of economic and ecological sustainability are being raised. A recent delegation of Chinese environmental scientists and economists visiting the World Resources Institute indicated that, in the decade since the chemical agricultural program began, ever greater amounts of chemicals are needed to keep productivity high. In some cases, productivity is slowly declining despite increasing inputs. Problems of pollution and erosion are reportedly widespread and the Chinese government is now sponsoring experiments and demonstrations based on reviving ecological agricultural methods. The system of farming that emerges from these swings of policy and technology will probably be a hybrid of biological and chemical-intensive approaches, and will be judged by a complex set of performance criteria. Certainly, yields per unit of land and labor will be extremely important. But long-term conservation of natural resources, stability of production, energy efficiency, and protection of human health will undoubtedly also be key criteria. Such criteria need not await dramatic increases or severe environmental degradation to be considered. A well-conceived agricultural development policy should treat sustainability and productivity as equally important goals.

To promote sustainable agriculture, advocates of an ecological approach must be prepared to analyze the appropriateness of any technology to specific sites and environmental conditions, not try to prescribe ready-made answers. When competing forms of agriculture—such as "organic" versus "conventional"—make conflicting claims about productivity and sustainability, ecological assessments will be needed, following the same set of criteria, to determine the strengths and weaknesses of both systems. Agroecologists must become arbiters in the debate on agriculture, not champions of one side.

Agroecologists must become arbiters in the debate on agriculture, not champions of one side.

Research

Agricultural research has historically emphasized maximizing production per unit of area and per unit of labor. In this industrial approach, research has been strongly biased toward advancing and refining the use of agricultural chemicals and farm machinery in monocultural systems. Not only ecologically questionable, this approach keeps agricultural scientists in industrialized and developing countries from formulating and answering certain key questions.

For years, agricultural research has become increasingly fragmented. Specialized disciplines often compete with each other for funds and public attention. Few ecologists work in agricultural schools or study in agricultural settings, and few agricultural scientists encounter basic ecological concepts within their own disciplines. This division of labor has left the agricultural sciences with little capability or interest in the overall functioning of agroecosystems as biological units. Countering this fragmentation, however, are several efforts to apply the techniques of systems science to agriculture. Integrated pest management (IPM), although generally limited to control of insects and other pests, was an early example.[167] IPM research has led, in some cases, to research on agroecosystem design and management as researchers try to identify optimal strategies for food production and environmental protection.[168] Cropping systems research and farming systems research have emerged within agricultural development as two responses to the Green Revolution technologies' apparent failure to reach the majority of farmers in developing countries. Both explore indigenous farmers' choices of technologies, cropping patterns, and other factors relating to food production. Farming systems research in particular tends to economic analysis and has found considerable support in agricultural development circles.[169] Agroecosystem research, pioneered by Imperial College's Gordon Conway, stems from an ecological point of view, though the system properties Conway has described—productivity, stability, sustainability, and equitability—are independent of any particular discipline.[170] Of these three applications of systems science, only agroecosystem research can encompass environmental considerations as well as economic and production criteria.

Many of the research centers funded by the World Bank, the U.S. Agency for International Development, and other assistance organizations through the Consultative Group for International Agricultural Research are now actively pursuing research programs on multiple cropping, especially aimed at improving low- or no-input agriculture. Development of farming systems research is particularly strong at some of these centers.[171] The Ford Foundation, a major force in the Green Revolution, has been one of the principal backers of Conway's agroecosystem analysis workshops, which have been instrumental in developing holistic approaches to agricultural research in Southeast Asia. An important outcome of this and related activities (especially those of the Environment and Policy Institute of the East-West Center) is a Southeast Asian Universities Agroecosystem Network, which coordinates and communicates research on agroecosystems throughout the region. Whether systems approaches such as these will significantly change the way agricultural research is funded and conducted remains to be seen. Certainly, systems approaches are important in the evolution of agricultural research, though they must explicitly focus on sustainability if progress is to be made. And agricultural scientists must be willing and able to pursue fundamental questions about the ecological basis of the systems they are studying.

Because of the paucity of research in agricultural ecology compared to production-oriented studies, a research agenda for the ecological approach to agricultural development is almost open-ended. One top agenda item will be to define and quantify basic terms of reference in agro-ecological investigations. New or refined methodologies are needed to measure soil quality, ecological efficiency, and rates of material and energy flows in agroecosystems. Such basic questions as why some crop combinations "overyield," how plants respond to insect damage or weed competition, why spatial arrangements of crop mixtures differ in their yields, and the role of soil micro-organisms in making nutrients available to plants need to be addressed. Ecological interactions such as the symbiotic relation between plants and mycorrhizal fungi (an association that can increase a plant's capacity to absorb nutrients by as much as 60 times[172]), resource-sharing among plants, predator/prey and parasite/host relationships that contribute to biological control of pests, and the role of plants' genetic diversity in the growth and spread of plant disease especially need further study. And finally, new strategies need to be developed to optimize land use through more effective cropping patterns, reduce losses due to insects and diseases, minimize competition from weeds, and maintain or improve soil fertility. These strategies' effectiveness must be quantified as much as possible, so that they will be widely adopted once proven sound in various environments.

National Agricultural Development Policies

The bias toward an industrial paradigm of agricultural development pervades not only research and education, but also the policies adopted by Third World governments seeking to increase agricultural productivity. Often, subsidies, pricing policies, infrastructures, and other supports provide incentives for input-intensive farming methods but not necessarily for more ecologically sustainable agriculture.

Why are so many agricultural policies aimed at maximizing, rather than optimizing, production? Many developing nations urgently need export earnings, so agricultural policies often stress maximum yield of such export crops as coffee, cotton, vegetables, and fruits. And because consumers expect many of these crops to be blemish-free, the fields, orchards, and plantations are usually treated heavily with chemical pesticides. Population pressure, especially in cities, boosts demand for food within developing countries ever higher, providing another rationale for maximizing yields. When governments accordingly stress yield per unit area, rather than yield per unit of input, farmers are often encouraged to abandon traditional methods, some of which may be valuable in developing more sustainable, productive farming systems.

One way that governments encourage farmers to use agricultural chemicals is to subsidize the prices of these inputs.[173] Sound management of pest and soil fertility should be based on the principle that the benefit (increased value of crop produced) of an input exceeds its cost. While a subsidy may result in production increases, it distorts the true economic value of the chemicals, so that optimal management is almost impossible. And subsidies offer no incentive to farmers who might increase production through nonchemical means, even though such alternatives may reduce environmental costs, which are rarely calculated in benefit/cost analyses of agricultural chemicals.

Food prices and land tenure have become key issues in agricultural development policy. How those issues are handled can affect the sustainability and productivity of agriculture. Artificially low food prices mean low productivity in many developing areas, most notably Africa, because such prices satisfy urban demand for cheap food without providing incentives for farmers to produce more. And if certain resource-conserving measures are perceived as more time-consuming or expensive than other means of production, farmers will be even less likely to adopt sustainable technologies when food prices are low. A recurring theme among those who encourage farmers to adopt resource-conserving practices is that farmers need a stake in the outcome of the project. The most frequently cited need is for land tenure. Most farmers who do not own their land and cannot pass it on to their children will not devote the time and effort needed to preserve the land. Clearly, sustainability can have meaning only to someone who can expect to farm a piece of land for many years, preferably for generations. Land ownership or, at a minimum, security of tenancy, must be part and parcel of any agricultural conservation efforts.

Policies regarding land use can also greatly affect the sustainability of agriculture. As the Nyabisindu case shows, some land should not be farmed at all, but left as forest to keep soil in place. Other land may be suitable for limited grazing even though it will not support cropping. And still other types of land might support such perennial crops as fruit trees or a combination of annual and perennial crops. The decision to develop a site for agriculture must be based on several factors, including slope, soil type, and the kind of farming methods to be used. Simplistic classification of land use solely determined by (for instance) slope is ineffective at best and counterproductive at worst.[174]

Development Assistance

Until recently, much of the effort in agricultural development assistance was geared toward producing export crops to help improve recipients' balance of payments. Where the assistance dealt with food production, it often emphasized larger scale, plantation-type projects. Today, many aid organizations are paying increasing attention to food production and to reaching "the poorest of the poor." Industrial agriculture is still favored, however, partly because of the orientation of the experts advising the assistance institutions. Moreover, to maximize production to meet rising demand, most development activities are concentrated where the agricultural potential is highest—namely, the fertile lowlands—which make up a very small percentage of most developing nations' total land area.

The sheer scale of development assistance can impede adoption of an ecological approach to agriculture. Projects conceived and executed on a national scale too often involve "top-down" designs of farming systems: little effort is made to fully understand specific sites. As a result, national infrastructural development—credit, marketing, and extension systems—often benefits lowland, input-intensive farmers more than their upland counterparts.[175]

Some signs of change are beginning to appear. The Nyabisindu project, for example, has been funded by the West German Agency for Technical Cooperation (GTZ), and several of the Sahelian agroforestry projects mentioned earlier were supported by the U.S. Agency for International Development (AID). AID may be getting more receptive— witness a multiple-objective research strategy announced in 1983, emphasizing sustained production in marginal environments, minimum-purchased-input production systems, cost-effective and environmentally acceptable pest management, and livestock in mixed-farming systems.[176] Another sign of change at AID is a program of small grants for research in innovative technologies[177] and a new policy to direct more project money through private voluntary organizations.[178] Sargent Shriver, the first director of the Peace Corps, believes "that AID is moving away from its emphasis on expensive infrastructure developments to the 'small is beautiful' philosophy" of the organization he helped found.[179] Time will tell whether these trends will persist and support an ecological approach to agricultural development, not only within AID and GTZ but throughout the development-assistance community.

The sheer scale of development assistance can impede adoption of an ecological approach to agriculture.

59

VI. An Action Plan for Sustainable Agriculture

Ecological Principles for Agricultural Development

In spite of the large information gaps, it is still possible to define principles that can guide agricultural development while research continues. Beginning with the concepts and observations discussed here, a general strategy can be described that will help move agriculture toward sustainability.

1. Soil Quality

General approaches toward sustainability can be gleaned from the principles and experience gained so far in agricultural ecology. Foremost among these are strategies for maintaining and improving soil quality. Agroecosystems can be designed to keep the soil covered with growing plants or crop residues for all or most of the year. Various multiple-cropping schemes not only accomplish this, but increase overall productivity of the land in the bargain. Where appropriate, maximum possible use should be made of perennial crops, so that the soil need be disturbed less often. Deep-rooted species should be utilized to create a net upward movement of soil nutrients. Perennials can also help protect the soil against wind and water erosion. Trees and shrubs should be included in agroecosystem designs to moderate the effects of drought, flooding, and severe temperatures. And all aspects of the farm system should take into account the need to return organic matter and biological sources of mineral nutrients to the soil.

2. Ecological Efficiency

Although efficiency in modern agriculture is most often couched in such economic terms as productivity of labor or cash inputs, ecological efficiency should also be considered. Ecosystems differ in the extent to which they utilize various resources, and knowledge about natural ecosystems can be used to help optimize agroecosystems' use of key factors. Systems that effectively recycle nutrients can both save money and avoid pollution. Where energy—whether from fuel, animals, or people—is scarce or expensive, energy efficiency should be sought in agroecosystem design. Concomitantly, strategies to improve energy efficiency may also enhance the efficiency with which other resources are used. For instance, cropping patterns that discourage weeds also reduce the need for cultivation or herbicide application. Using resistant plant varieties and encouraging biological control of insects minimize the use of costly pesticides. Multilayered crop canopies capture larger percentages of solar energy, raising land productivity as well. And relying at least in part on biological sources of nitrogen and other nutrients reduces the need to purchase fossil-fuel-derived fertilizers.

3. Agroecosystem Stability

Stable ecosystems are characterized by various internal checks and balances—"negative feedback," as described earlier. Generally, short feedback loops are more stabilizing than long ones. In other words, management actions that take place soon after a problem is recognized will most likely correct the situation before it becomes a crisis. By the same token, if problems go undiagnosed or corrective actions are not undertaken promptly, the system can veer too far from its intended "course" to set aright.

Agroecosystem designs finely tuned to the local environment are likely to include more naturally occurring negative feedback loops, such as predators and parasites of insect pests. Farming practices can also be selected to help stabilize cropping systems. Methods are needed to help farmers monitor their fields and determine the status of crops, soils, pests, and other aspects of the agroecosystem. And methods must be available to respond to changes in the environment—weather shifts, pest damage, etc.—that help restore balance in the system. For instance, crop varieties that can be planted very late in the growing season and still produce an acceptable yield could be valuable in areas subject to occasional, unpredictable floods.

4. Diversity

Diversity, a cornerstone of the ecosystem paradigm for agricultural development, needs to be further studied and refined. The research conducted so far indicates that several kinds of diversity are important. Complex spatial arrangements of crops help make the best use of available nutrients, water, and sunlight. Diversity of crops in time can extend growing seasons and assure adequate ground cover as protection against wind and water erosion. And genetic variability both within and among crop species often helps provide natural protection against pests.

Naturally occurring diversity in wilderness ecosystems serves no "purpose" in the sense that its human-directed counterpart does in agroecosystems, but it does represent an irreplaceable resource for future agriculture. The species mix in natural ecosystems may offer biological-control agents, new crops, genetic material for hybridization, and biochemicals for enhancing productivity. Traditional crop varieties represent another genetic reserve that must be protected from extinction. Research programs, economic development policies, and conser-

Naturally occurring diversity in wilderness ecosystems serves no "purpose" in the sense that its human-directed counterpart does in agroecosystems, but it does represent an irreplaceable resource for future agriculture.

vation efforts all need to be designed with these agricultural resources in mind.

Development Criteria

To assure that ecological principles are followed in agricultural development, assistance organizations need to establish measurable criteria for judging proposed projects. The conditions for sustainable agriculture as discussed in Chapter III spell out just such a set of criteria:

1. Replenishment of soil nutrients removed by crops;
2. Maintenance of the soil's physical condition;
3. Constant or increasing humus level in the soil;
4. No build up of weeds, pests, or diseases;
5. No increase in soil acidity or toxic elements;
6. Control of soil erosion;
7. Minimization of off-farm contamination of the environment;
8. Maintenance of adequate habitat for wildlife; and
9. Conservation of genetic resources.

Project proposals should be required to show how these criteria will be met. If a project requires purchasing such inputs as fertilizers and pesticides, means for minimizing their environmental effects should be spelled out. Assessments of the reliability of supply and stability of agrochemical prices should be conducted prior to funding. How indigenous resources can be substituted for imported industrial inputs should be explicitly considered. Proposals should also detail how the project will be monitored to make sure that the above criteria are being met and should include a budget for conducting the monitoring.

Assessing Agriculture's Sustainability

Considerable debate has occurred since the early 1970s on industrialized agriculture's sustainability. With their vast capital investments and ability to pay for imported fossil-fuel-based inputs, farmers in the developed countries may have seemed immune to the problems of environmental degradation, loss of genetic diversity, and maintenance of soil fertility that face the developing world. Now a different kind of crisis—an economic one—is causing some farmers in the United States and elsewhere to take another look at alternative farming practices to cut costs.[180] But the ecological constraints facing agriculture must be faced—if not now, then in the next oil shock. Agriculture in the industrialized world will have to confront its environmental effects and resource dependencies, and new forms of production are certain to emerge.[181]

The time has come for a global assessment of agriculture's sustainability. Clearly the issues are different in developed and developing countries, and they also differ among areas within those two groups. But the unifying element is the set of ecological concepts discussed here. A region-by-region "agroecological audit" should be conducted, covering energy efficiency, soil conservation and regeneration, nutrient sources and uses, preservation of genetic diversity, stability of yields, water use and hydrology, off-farm contamination, effects on natural areas, and similar topics. The United Nations is the logical sponsor for such an analysis, with the Food and Agriculture Organization (FAO), the U.N. Environment Programme and the World Bank involved. These agencies, along with other development-assistance institutions, could contract with leading agricultural scientists and ecologists to carry out the study. For detailed assessments of farming practices and resources, the International Agricultural Research Centers that have already begun programs in farming systems research and related studies could contribute significantly. This assessment should re-examine the assumptions in the FAO food-security study *Land, Food and People* that low (industrial-based) inputs mean low productivity and high inputs equate with high productivity. The agroecological audit would see how countries and regions really can provide food on a sustained basis relying principally on indigenous resources for fertility and pest management.

The purpose of the audit would be to identify principal problem areas by region, in terms of both productivity and sustainability, and to provide a basis for developing coordinated, comprehensive research programs and policy changes to meet those twin needs. The audit could be duplicated at the national level, either in concert with or following upon the global assessment. Bilateral and multilateral assistance organizations should provide funds for these national audits to be carried out. In this way, the resources, constraints, and problems of agriculture can be addressed systematically, incorporating both production and environmental considerations in one integrated program. Without such an overall assessment, it may be difficult to convince decision-makers of the need for research and development in sustainable agriculture.

Research and Education

Conduct studies to compare farming systems' productivity and sustainability.

As research and development progress in both high-input and low-input agriculture, comparative studies of the various agroecosystem designs should be carried out to determine their strengths and shortcomings vis-a-vis long-term productivity and sustainability. The research must be conducted under many environmental and sociological settings where the new agroecosystem designs are likely to be implemented, including productive lowland areas (where most past research has been done) and marginally productive upland regions (where the majority of subsistence farmers are).

Involve traditional farmers in setting research priorities and testing new techniques.

Successful agricultural development requires the active participation of the farmers who are supposed to benefit from technological innovation.[182] Agricultural ecologists have learned to respect the inherent wisdom in much traditional practice. Involving the ultimate "clients" of agricultural research in both the design and testing of improved technologies serves two objectives. First, it allows specialists to capture some of the practical knowledge about local agroecosystems. Second, it offers greater assurance that new methods will be more widely adopted once their effectiveness has been demonstrated.

Design and develop equipment for use in mixed-crop farming systems.

One drawback of many mixed-crop farming systems is that they are difficult to mechanize.[183] Where labor is a limiting factor in farm operations, appropriate machinery is needed that can operate effectively in a polyculture's complex environment. Designers need to come up with safe and durable hand-held and animal-drawn equipment that can be locally manufactured and repaired, easily operated and maintained. A multi-purpose tool bar developed in Botswana which is made of scrap materials and can be used for cultivation, planting, and weeding exemplifies indigenous technological innovation that meets smallholders' needs.[184] Where pesticides are needed, hand-held applicators are being developed that use minimal amounts of chemicals, are safe to use, and keep environmental contamination to a minimum.[185] In general, research on mechanization should optimize rather than minimize animal power and human labor, taking into account farmers' available labor supply and cash, alternative sources of employment, and the role of draft animals in the ecology and economy of the local farming community.

Conduct studies of traditional crop varieties and natural relatives of crop species.

Information is a key to preventing the loss of irreplaceable genetic resources. Ethno-botanical studies are needed in areas where traditional farming is still widely practiced to learn new uses for wild and domesticated plants. Ecological studies in natural habitats need to be expanded to improve understanding of the wide array of traits available in wild species. Such studies can also reveal new insights into the interactions between crops and their pests. In the absence of chemical pesticides and other human intervention, the population dynamics of insects, plant pathogens, and other potential pests can be quite different from those found in highly managed agroecosystems.

Careful study of these species in undisturbed natural settings can reveal much about how best to manage them in agriculture.

Include ecologists in the design and implementation of agricultural research programs.

For agroecology to become a fully recognized field of study, ecology must become integrated into agricultural science. In universities and research centers where team approaches are already being used to improve agriculture, ecologists should be part of such teams, both as specialists in the ecological dimensions of the projects and as key resources for bringing the various disciplines together. Where teams or systems approaches are not yet being employed, ecologists can catalyze interdisciplinary studies.

The need for multi- and bi-lateral development assistance agencies to support appropriate national and international agricultural research is plain. Aid organizations can provide funds to train and hire agroecologists into agricultural research organizations and to support research initiatives based on ecological analyses of developing countries' farming systems. The research centers that belong to the Consultative Group for International Agricultural Research (CGIAR) should be encouraged by the various donor organizations to add broader ecological considerations to their research agendas. CGIAR and its donors might also consider creating a new center to further the study of agroecology. Such a center could then serve as a resource for all of the members, conducting research on basic theoretical and methodological issues that concern investigators working in all kinds of environments.

Indigenous agroecological expertise in developing countries is especially important to improve communication between farmers and scientists and to provide long-term continuity in national research programs. National and international networks of agroecologists deserve expanded support as a means of training and sustaining these scientists in their work.

Develop agroecology curricula for agricultural colleges.

If an ecological approach to improving agriculture is to take hold, a new generation of scientists will have to be trained for the job. In particular, interdisciplinary undergraduate and graduate programs in agricultural ecology are needed in agricultural schools. Such curricula could turn out agroecologists for the decades to come and offer in-service training for working scientists and agricultural officials trying to improve the sustainability of farming. Funds for developing these programs in agricultural colleges should come from national and international organizations concerned with science education.

National Agricultural Development Policies

Encourage local economic and agronomic decision-making.

Detailed knowledge of the specific characteristics of the farm site is essential to effective system design and management. Understanding local needs and demand for products can lead to crop mixes that assure marketability throughout the year. And experience with variations in labor supply and demand can contribute to farm systems that provide employment and avoid labor shortfalls at critical periods. Most likely, letting farmers and local agricultural advisors make their own decisions based on local conditions will encourage development of indigenous resources for soil fertility and pest management. Where fertilizers and other external inputs are needed, keeping supply lines short is the only way to make sure that the materials are available at the appropriate times in crop cycles.

Such local control can be enhanced by farmer/consumer cooperatives, locally managed credit systems, and small facilities for producing needed agricultural inputs (using locally available resources where possible). Creating and supporting local and intra-regional marketing systems would support the preservation of indigenous crop varieties by helping to retain local food preferences as well as providing an outlet for goods. Such development would also facilitate seed exchange among farmers, a common practice in traditional agriculture that helps keep genetic diversity high within and among fields.[186]

Encourage use of biological means of fertility management and pest control by removing subsidies on agricultural chemicals.

Although agricultural chemicals can often enhance productivity, their use should reflect their true costs. Subsidizing these costs can encourage overuse and misuse, with potentially serious effects on human health and the environment. In many instances, governments are spending enormous sums of money for subsidies without monitoring actual benefits to the agricultural economy.[187]

These funds would, in the long term, be more effective if used to make more diagnostic and advisory services available to farmers. Such services could include soil-fertility analysis, marketing advice, pest population monitoring, and assistance in selecting crop varieties and designing efficient cropping patterns.

Money now going into subsidies could also be channeled into support for farmers to help them make long-term improvements to their land. Government funds could be paid to those farmers who take steps to reduce soil erosion, improve soil quality, and reduce pollution of nearby water supplies since these actions benefit the society as a whole.

Give effective land tenure to farmers who demonstrate that they are conserving resources.

Although land reform is a prime requisite for promoting sustainable agriculture in the developing world, simply making land available or conferring ownership is not enough to guarantee that the land will be farmed in an ecologically sound fashion. Clearly, education and advisory support will be needed to help farmers manage their land effectively. Tenure on the land could, in fact, be conditional on adoption of *proven* means for conserving soil, water, and other natural resources. Such a policy could prevent land-reform programs from being subverted by speculators or others who have no long-term stake in the viability of the land for farming.

Encourage farmer participation in planning and implementing agricultural development projects.

Sustainable agroecosystem design and management requires programs of education for farmers that emphasize their independence rather than their reliance on outside expertise. Conventional extension practice, in contrast, often has a "top-down" bias.[188] Designers of agricultural development projects must consider the farmer a rational decision-maker who in a certain sense knows more about the overall system being managed than they do. Certainly, improvements in traditional farming practices are possible and necessary, but such improvements must be offered to farmers as choices or sets of options, for farmers to consider along with all the other constraints and opportunities that they face.

Including farmers in the planning and execution of development projects increases the chances that proposed improvements in agricultural methods will fit the locales where they will be introduced. Farmers' involvement in development planning can also help provide continuity with traditional agriculture by encouraging farmer-to-farmer communication—often, the best way to spread new ideas and methods.[189]

Tailor development projects and policies to specific agroecological zones.

Governmental economic planners must take into account the different capabilities and needs of upland and lowland agriculture when designing development projects. Farming methods and performance criteria may differ considerably in the two areas. The goals of development will thus be quite distinct as well. Maintaining productivity while improving sustainability may be the objective in the lowlands, while increasing productivity without sacrificing sustainability may be the goal in the uplands. Soil erosion may be the priority in hilly areas, while pest management may be more important in the high-value commercial crops in the fertile lowlands. Rural social services may be essential to upland agricultural development projects, while credit may be of greater significance to lowland farmers. Sustainable agriculture is the result of a combination of locale-specific ecological, economic, and social factors, and efforts to improve the lot of farmers must be fine tuned if they are to succeed in the long term.

International Programs

Incorporate environmental criteria into economic analyses of development programs.

Continuing and further developing the initiative begun by (among others) AID and the World Bank, development-assistance agencies should routinely include environmental considerations in cost-benefit analyses of proposed development projects. In these assessments, such agricultural resources as soil, water, crop genetic resources, and species beneficial to pest management should be included along with wildlife and wilderness concerns. In addition, agricultural development should be analyzed as a potential cause of environmental degradation, including soil runoff, siltation of waterways, pollution from agricultural chemicals, habitat destruction, and depletion of genetic resources.

As important as such cost-benefit analyses are, they occur before final funding decisions are made. Post-funding monitoring and evaluation of development projects are at least as urgently needed. For each project, recipients and donors need specific criteria for determining if natural resources essential to agricultural sustainability are being properly managed. In addition, corrective measures (or procedures for developing them) need to be spelled out in advance so recipients and donors know what to do if environmental criteria are not being met.

These environmental considerations should also be included in the basic macroeconomic analyses and planning operations of the development-assistance agencies.

Design special program strategies to deal with development of upland or marginal agricultural lands.

Since uplands and other marginally productive areas comprise most agricultural land in the developing world, and because the ecology and social structure of farming in these areas usually differ considerably from agriculture in fertile lowlands, agricultural development will require new approaches if it is to succeed in the long term. In general, a strategy for these areas will include a focus on small-scale farming closer in style to traditional methods than the more input-intensive Green Revolution approach. The wide variability in conditions from locale to locale suggests a development strategy based on many small-scale projects rather than a few larger ones. Accordingly, development advisors should encourage farmers who accept high-yielding varieties to mix them with traditional varieties in their cropping systems, rather than replacing the old strains with the new. This may be the only effective means for improving crop genetics without losing all-important local adaptability.

To succeed, such strategies must rely on an "adaptive feedback" approach to project design and implementation, rather than formulas. Researchers and advisors need to find out which traditional agricultural methods have "survival value" to farmers and why, and then set out to introduce improvements that do not compromise this essential characteristic. Anthropologists can, in many circumstances, provide an invaluable link between scientists and traditional farmers, eliciting and interpreting information about farming practices that can give clues to future development potential.

These strategies point to a policy that may often favor funding projects through private voluntary organizations and other nongovernmental avenues. Although this approach may give some donor and host governments pause, it may be the only way to assure that projects are properly attuned to the specific sites where they are being carried out.

Include traditional farming systems within the framework of ecosystem-conservation efforts.

Conservation measures must take agricultural resources and wild species into account when preservation programs are planned. As industrial technologies come to pervade agriculture in developing countries, the genetic diversity maintained in traditional farming systems is often rapidly lost. And the ecological understanding inherent in indigenous technologies can disappear as well, to be recovered only through painstaking effort, if at all. One response to the declining diversity of planted crops is to maintain and expand seed collections, but preservation of the farming systems themselves conserves not only the germplasm in traditional varieties but also the information about their traits (including, say, resistance to pests or drought). The latter strategy also allows the crop varieties to continue to evolve in response to natural stresses and constraints.

Wildlife and allied conservation efforts need to incorporate traditional farming systems and indigenous crop varieties within their scope of concern, as is done to some extent by the Biosphere Reserves Program of UNESCO. Only by recognizing the continuities between agriculture and wild ecosystems can we hope to preserve either effectively.

Conclusion

Agriculture passed a turning point with the energy crises of the 1970s. After decades of development based on the assumption of continous supplies of cheap oil, agriculturists began to realize that they live in a finite world where limiting factors are physical and economic realities. Out of that realization has emerged a new appreciation of natural systems' ability to utilize their environments efficiently and in equilibrium with available resources.

With continuing population increases and rising food demand, industrial agriculture will not and should not disappear. But an ecological approach can begin to redress the environmental deterioration that both industrial agriculture and misplaced traditional agriculture have brought about. Carefully planned, managed, and monitored, multiple cropping may also begin to give developing countries the productive edge they must have to feed at least a significant portion of their populations with indigenous resources on a continuing basis.

Policy-makers must be willing to take hold of the ecological approach and make it their own. They must ask whether the structure of land tenure in their countries gives farmers the incentive to conserve soil. They must raise the difficult question of whether food self-sufficiency is ecologically sustainable with internal resources. They must ask whether fertilizer and pesticide subsidies are effective tools for developing a stable agriculture. And they must choose between developing large, expensive manufacturing facilities for agricultural inputs and creating an agriculture that depends less on those inputs. The choices are hard, and the answers far from clear-cut. Nonetheless, as we come to better understand the ecological basis of our food supply, we also realize more and more that such decisions will have to be made before nature makes them for us.

Dr. Michael Dover is an adjunct associate of the World Resources Institute. Trained as an ecologist, he has specialized in pest and pesticide management at Michigan State University and the U.S. Environmental Protection Agency. As an Associate at WRI from 1983–1985, Dr. Dover wrote two policy studies for the project on Global Pesticide Use. Currently, he is a consultant in Peterborough, New Hampshire.

Dr. Lee Talbot is an ecologist with experience on resource and environmental issues in more than 100 countries. Formerly, he was Director-General of the International Union for Conservation of Nature and Natural Resources, and was Chief Scientist of the President's Council on Environmental Quality. He is a Visiting Fellow with the World Resources Institute, consultant to the World Bank, and Fellow with the East-West Center, Hawaii.

Notes

1. Sylvan H. Wittwer, "Crop Productivity—Research Imperatives: A Decade of Change," prepared for International Conference on Crop Productivity—Research Imperatives Revisited, Boyne Highlands, Michigan, October 1985. Wittwer, one of the convenors of the conference, is Director Emeritus of the Michigan Agricultural Experiment Station.

2. *Ibid.*

3. United Nations Food and Agriculture Organization, *Land, Food and People* (Rome: Food and Agriculture Organization, 1984).

4. The assumptions embodied in the FAO report—for example, that all arable land would be used for food production, and that the agricultural technologies most likely to maximize yields would be those based on the Western European model—are clearly unrealistic. Hence, the most optimistic projections are either unattainable or, worse, would cause massive environmental and social disruption if achieved. Nonetheless, the study does point to the magnitude of the need to provide adequate nutrition for a rapidly growing global population. And because of the problems associated with the medium- and high-technology scenarios, the low-technology scenario—FAO's most pessimistic projection—may be the only believable one.

5. Y.H. Yang, "Nutritional and Environmental Considerations in Small-scale Intensive Food Production," presented at the Second International Conference on Small Scale Intensive Food Production, Santa Barbara, California, October 1981.

6. Kenneth A. Dahlberg, *Beyond the Green Revolution: The Ecology and Politics of Global Agricultural Development* (New York: Plenum Press, 1979).

7. William S. Saint and E. Walter Coward, Jr., "Agriculture and Behavioral Science: Emerging Orientations," *Science* 197 (1977): 733–737.

8. Wittwer, ''Crop Productivity—Research Imperatives: A Decade of Change.''

9. Michael J. Dover, *A Better Mousetrap: Improving Pest Management for Agriculture* (Washington, D.C.: World Resources Institute, 1985); Robert F. Wasserstrom and Richard Wiles, *Field Duty: U.S. Farmworkers and Pesticide Safety* (Washington, D.C.: World Resources Institute, 1985); Michael Dover and Brian Croft, *Getting Tough: Public Policy and the Management of Pesticide Resistance* (Washington, D.C.: World Resources Institute, 1984).

10. The meanings of the terms ''ecosystem'' and ''agroecosystem'' are considered at length in later chapters. Here, the ecosystem is considered the entire array of biotic interactions that occur within an ecologically distinct site. An agroecosystem is a special type of ecosystem that includes farming.

11. G.F. Wilson and B.T. Kang, ''Developing Stable and Productive Biological Cropping Systems for the Humid Tropics,'' in B. Stonehouse, ed., *Biological Husbandry: A Scientific Approach to Organic Farming* (London: Butterworths, 1981), pp. 193–203.

12. Office of Technology Assessment, *Innovative Biological Technologies for Lesser Developed Countries—Workshop Proceedings* (Washington, D.C.: U.S. Congress, Office of Technology Assessment, OTA-BP-F-29, July 1985).

13. *Ibid.*

14. Robert Rodale, ''The Past and Future of Regenerative Agriculture,'' in T.C. Edens, C. Fridgen and S.L. Battenfield, eds., *Sustainable Agriculture and Integrated Farming Systems* (East Lansing, Mich.: Michigan State University Press, 1985), pp. 312–17.

15. A. Terry Rambo and Percy E. Sajise, ''Developing a Regional Network for Interdisciplinary Research on Rural Ecology,'' *The Environmental Professional* 7 (1985): 289–98.

16. Miguel A. Altieri, *Agroecology: The Scientific Basis of Alternative Agriculture* (Berkeley, Calif.: Division of Biological Control, University of California, 1983); Stephen R. Gliessman, ''Economic and Ecological Factors in Designing and Managing Sustainable Agroecosystems,'' in Edens et al., *Sustainable Agriculture and Integrated Farming Systems,* pp. 56–63; Richard Lowrance, Benjamin R. Stinner, and Garfield House, eds., *Agricultural Ecosystems: Unifying Concepts* (New York: John Wiley and Sons, 1984); Gordon R. Conway, ''What is an Agroecosystem and Why is it Worthy of Study?'' in A. Terry Rambo and Percy E. Sajise, eds., *An Introduc-*

tion to Human Ecology Research on Agricultural Systems in Southeast Asia (College, Laguna: University of the Philippines at Los Baños, 1984), pp. 25–38.

17. Altieri, *Agroecology*; Gordon R. Conway, "Agroecosystem Analysis," *Agricultural Administration* 20 (1985): 1–25; George W. Cox and Michael D. Atkins, *Agricultural Ecology* (San Francisco: W.H. Freeman and Sons, 1979); G.E. Dalton, *Study of Agricultural Systems* (London: Applied Sciences, 1975); O.L. Loucks, "Emergence of Research on Agroecosystems," *Annual Review of Ecology and Systematics* 8 (1977): 173–92; Lowrance et al., *Agricultural Ecosystems*; C.R.W. Spedding, *The Biology of Agricultural Systems* (New York: Academic Press, 1978).

18. Richard B. Norgaard, "Sociosystem and Ecosystem Coevolution in the Amazon," *Journal of Environmental Economics and Management* 8 (1981): 238–54.

19. Thomas C. Edens and Herman E. Koenig, "Agroecosystem Management in a Resource-Limited World," *BioScience* 30 (1980): 697–701; Richard B. Norgaard, "Coevolutionary Agricultural Development," *Economic Development and Cultural Change* 32 (1984): 524–46; E.F. Schumacher, *Small is Beautiful: Economics as if People Mattered* (New York: Harper and Row, 1973).

20. Not all developing areas are in the tropics, but a great many are. Because much environmental disruption in development stems from the disparity between temperate-zone practices and tropical ecology, this paper focusses mainly on tropical agriculture, but the principles discussed can be applied to agricultural development in any environment.

21. Suraphol Ratanasophon, "Tropical Soils and Agriculture," presented at Workshop on Human Ecology, Khon Kaen, Thailand, April–May 1983.

22. World Resources Institute and International Institute for Environment and Development, *World Resources 1986* (New York: Basic Books, 1986).

23. Jen-Hu Chang, "Tropical Agriculture: Crop Diversity and Crop Yields," *Economic Geography* 53 (1977): 241–54.

24. *Ibid.*

25. R.W.J. Keay, "Temperate and Tropical: Some Comparisons and Contrasts," in J.G. Hawkes, ed., *Conservation and Agriculture* (Montclair, N.J.: Allanheld, Osmun and Co., 1978), pp. 243–48.

26. E.P. Odum, *Fundamentals of Ecology* (Philadelphia: W.B. Saunders Co., 1971).

27. T. Arnason et al., "Decline in Soil Fertility Due to Intensification of Land Use by Shifting Agriculturists in Belize, Central America," *Agro-Ecosystems* 8 (1982): 27–37.

28. P.S. Ramakrishnan and O.P. Toky, "Soil Nutrient Status of Hill Agro-Ecosystems and Recovery Pattern After Slash and Burn Agriculture (*Jhum*) in North-Eastern India," *Plant and Soil* 60 (1981): 41–64.

29. Mostafa K. Tolba, *Earth Matters: Environmental Challenges for the 1980s* (Nairobi: United Nations Environment Programme, 1983).

30. Norman Myers, *Conversion of Tropical Moist Forests* (Washington, D.C.: National Academy Press, 1980).

31. Tolba, *Earth Matters*.

32. Myers, *Conversion of Tropical Moist Forests*.

33. Betty C. Abregana et al., "Comprehensive Small-Scale Upland Agroforestry: An Alternative to Shifting Cultivation in the Balin-sasayao Rainforest Region, Negros Oriental, Philippines," report submitted to the Ford Foundation, Silliman University, January 1983.

34. Percy E. Sajise, "Regeneration of Critical Upland Areas: An Ecological Imperative," presented at the University of the Philippines at Los Baños, January 1977; Percy E. Sajise, "Grassland Regeneration Strategy for Small Upland Farmers," presented at the University of the Philippines at Los Baños, July 1980.

35. Tolba, *Earth Matters*.

36. Abregana et al., "Comprehensive Small-Scale Upland Agroforestry."

37. Sajise, "Regeneration of Critical Upland Areas."

38. Wittwer, "Crop Productivity—Research Imperatives: A Decade of Change."

39. Tolba, *Earth Matters*.

40. P.A. Sanchez, *Properties and Management of Soils in the Tropics* (New York: John Wiley and Sons, 1976).

41. Tolba, *Earth Matters.*

42. Sam H. Johnson III, ''Temporal Land Resource Concerns and Farming Systems Research: Chiang Mai Valley, Northern Thailand,'' *Land Economics* 60 (1984): 202–10.

43. David Pimentel, ed., *World Food, Pest Losses, and the Environment* (Boulder, Colo.: Westview Press, 1978).

44. Daniel H. Janzen, ''Tropical Agroecosystems,'' *Science* 182 (1973): 1212–19; Martin Kellman, ''Some Implications of Biotic Interactions for Sustained Tropical Agriculture,'' *Proceedings of the Association of American Geographers* 6 (1974): 142–45.

45. Arnason et al., ''Decline in Soil Fertility Due to Intensification of Land Use''; K. Moody, ''Weeds and Shifting Cultivation,'' *PANS* 21 (1975): 188–94.

46. ''A Look at World Pesticide Markets,'' *Farm Chemicals* (September 1981): 55–60; William J. Storck, ''Pesticides Head for Recovery,'' *Chemical and Engineering News* 62 (April 9, 1984): 35–59.

47. Tolba, *Earth Matters.*

48. Moody, ''Weeds and Shifting Cultivation.''

49. Dover, *A Better Mousetrap.*

50. Gordon R. Conway and David S. McCauley, ''Intensifying Tropical Agriculture: The Indonesian Experience,'' *Nature* 302 (1983): 288–89.

51. Dover, *A Better Mousetrap.*

52. Dover and Croft, *Getting Tough.*

53. Dover, *A Better Mousetrap.*

54. Miguel A. Altieri, ''Developing Pest Management Strategies for Small Farmers Based on Traditional Knowledge,'' *Bulletin of the Institute for Development Anthropology* 3 (1985): 13–18.

55. Ranil Senanayake, ''The Ecological, Energetic, and Agronomic Systems of Ancient and Modern Sri Lanka,'' in Gordon K. Douglass, ed., *Agricultural Sustainability in a Changing World Order* (Boulder, Colo.: Westview Press, 1984), pp. 227–37.

56. *Ibid.*

57. Douglass, "The Meanings of Agricultural Sustainability," in Douglass, *Agricultural Sustainability in a Changing World Order*, pp. 3–29.

58. Gliessman, "Economic and Ecological Factors in Designing and Managing Sustainable Agroecosystems."

59. S.J. Holt and L.M. Talbot, "New Principles for the Conservation of Wild Living Resources," *Wildlife Monographs* No. 59 (1978).

60. J.H. Beverton and S.J. Holt, *On the Dynamics of Exploited Fish Populations* (Great Britain, Ministry of Agriculture, Fisheries, and Food: Fishery Investigations, Series II, Vol. XIX, 1957); W.E. Ricker, "Handbook of Computations for Biological Statistics of Fish Populations," *Bulletin of the Fisheries Research Board of Canada* 119 (1958): 1–300; Lawrence B. Slobodkin, *Growth and Regulation of Animal Populations* (New York: Holt, Rinehart and Winston, 1961); E.P. Odum, *Fundamentals of Ecology* (Philadelphia: W.B. Saunders Co., 1971).

61. D.J. Greenland, "Bringing the Green Revolution to the Shifting Cultivator," *Science* 190 (1975): 841–44.

62. Robert D. Hart and Antonio M. Pinchinat, "Integrative Agricultural Systems Research," presented at the Inter-Caribbean Seminar on Farming Systems Research Methodology, Pointe-a-Pitre, Guadeloupe, May 1980; Conway, "What is an Agroecosystem and Why is it Worthy of Study?"

63. Although an *economic* argument might be made for simply keeping such dependence at an affordable level, an *ecological* view of agriculture supports the notion that a sustainable agriculture should rely on renewable resources wherever possible.

64. Charles J. Krebs, *Ecology: The Experimental Analysis of Distribution and Abundance* (New York: Harper and Row, 1972).

65. Ramon Margalef, *Perspectives in Ecological Theory* (Chicago: University of Chicago Press, 1968).

66. Robert H. Whittaker, *Communities and Ecosystems* (New York: Macmillan, 1970).

67. L.R. Clark, R.L. Kitching, and P.W. Geier, "On the Scope and Value of Ecology," *Protection Ecology* 1 (1978/1979): 223–43.

68. Margalef, *Perspectives in Ecological Theory*; Eugene P. Odum, "The Strategy of Ecosystem Development," *Science* 164 (1969): 262–70; Odum, *Fundamentals of Ecology*.

69. G.E. Likens, F.H. Bormann, and N.M. Johnson, ''Nitrofication: Importance to Nutrient Losses From a Cutover Forested Eco-system,'' *Science* 163 (1969): 1205–6.

70. Odum, *Fundamentals of Ecology.*

71. Robert D. Hart, ''A Natural Ecosystem Analog Approach to the Design of a Successional Crop System for Tropical Forest Environments,'' *Biotropica* 12 (Supplement on Tropical Succession, 1980): 73–82.

72. Linda Christanty Widagda, ''An Ecosystem Analysis of West-Javanese Home Gardens,'' mimeo, Environment and Policy Institute, East-West Center, Honolulu, Hawaii, June 1981.

73. For example, see G. Evelyn Hutchinson, ''Homage to Santa Rosalia, or Why Are There So Many Different Kinds of Animals?'' *American Naturalist* 93 (1959): 145–59; Lawrence B. Slobodkin and Howard L. Sanders, ''On the Contribution of Environmental Predictability to Species Diversity,'' in G.M. Woodwell and H.H. Smith, eds., *Diversity and Stability in Ecological Systems* (Upton, N.Y.: Brookhaven National Laboratory, 1969 Brookhaven Symposia in Biology No. 22), pp. 82–95.

74. E.O. Wilson and W.H. Bossert, *A Primer of Population Biology* (Stamford, Conn.: Sinauer Associates, 1971); K.E.F. Watt, *Principles of Environmental Science* (New York: McGraw-Hill, 1973); E. Goldsmith et al., ''A Blueprint for Survival. Introduction: The Need for Change,'' *Ecologist* 2: 2–7; Rene Dubos, *Man Adapting* (New Haven, Conn.: Yale University Press, 1965).

75. Charles S. Elton, *The Ecology of Invasions by Animals and Plants* (London: Methuen, 1958); Robert H. MacArthur, ''Fluctuations of Animal Populations, and a Measure of Community Stability,'' *Ecology* 36 (1955): 533–36.

76. Daniel Goodman, ''The Theory of Diversity-Stability Relationships in Ecology,'' *Quarterly Review of Biology* 50 (1975): 237–66.

77. Raymond F. Dasmann, John P. Milton, and Peter H. Freeman, *Ecological Principles for Economic Development* (New York: John Wiley and Sons, 1973).

78. A. Gomez-Pompa, C. Vasquez-Yanes, and S. Guevara, ''The Tropical Rain Forest: A Non-Renewable Resource,'' *Science* 177 (1972): 762–65; Michael J. Dover, *The Effect of a Mowing Perturbation on the Arthropod Component of Old-Field Communities: A Field Test of the Diversity-Stability Hypothesis,* unpublished Ph.D. Dissertation, State University of New York at Stony Brook, 1975.

79. Dover, *A Field Test of the Diversity-Stability Hypothesis*; L.E. Hurd et al., "Stability and Diversity at Three Trophic Levels in Terrestrial Ecosystems," *Science* 173 (1971): 1134–36; L.E. Hurd and L.L. Wolf, "Stability in Relation to Nutrient Enrichment in Arthropod Consumers of Old-Field Successional Ecosystems," *Ecological Monographs* 44 (1974): 465–82; N.G. Hairston et al., "The Relationship Between Species Diversity and Stability: An Experimental Approach with Protozoa and Bacteria," *Ecology* 49 (1968): 1091–1101; W.W. Murdoch et al., "Diversity and Pattern in Plants and Insects," *Ecology* 51 (1972): 497–502.

80. Robert M. May, *Stability and Complexity in Model Ecosystems* (Princeton, N.J.: Princeton University Press, 1973); Goodman, "The Theory of Diversity-Stability Relationships in Ecology,"; Krebs, *Ecology*.

81. Slobodkin and Sanders, "On the Contribution of Environmental Predictability to Species Diversity"; D.J. Futuyma, "Community Structure and Stability in Constant Environments," *American Naturalist* 107 (1973): 443–46.

82. Dover, *A Field Test of the Diversity-Stability Hypothesis*.

83. *Ibid*.

84. Ramon Margalef, "Diversity and Stability: A Practical Proposal and a Model of Interdependence," in Woodwell and Smith, *Diversity and Stability in Ecological Systems*, pp. 25–37.

85. Dover, *A Field Test of the Diversity-Stability Hypothesis*.

86. Margalef, "Diversity and Stability: A Practical Proposal and a Model of Interdependence."

87. C.S. Holling, "Resilience and Stability of Ecological Systems," *Annual Review of Ecology and Systematics* 4 (1973): 1–23.

88. Dover, *A Field Test of the Diversity-Stability Hypothesis*.

89. May, *Stability and Complexity in Model Ecosystems*; Krebs, *Ecology*; R.C. Lewontin, "The Meaning of Stability," in Woodwell and Smith, *Diversity and Stability in Ecological Systems*, pp. 13–24.

90. R.M. May, "Stability in Multispecies Community Models," *Mathematical Bioscience* 12 (1971): 59–79.

91. Conway, "Agroecosystem Analysis."

92. *Ibid.* Conway uses the term "stability" as "persistence" is used here, and "sustainability" to mean the same thing as resilience. As often happens in discussions of stability, no distinction is made between resistance and resilience. This is unfortunate, since in agriculture, the planning and design strategies may be quite different for the two characteristics. It is also probably a higher priority to minimize change (that is, avoid interruption of output) than to design for recovery.

93. Slobodkin, *Growth and Regulation of Animal Populations.*

94. *Ibid.*

95. Odum, *Fundamentals of Ecology.*

96. John M. Street, "An Evaluation of the Concept of Carrying Capacity," *Professional Geographer* 21 (1969): 104–107.

97. R.H. MacArthur and E.O. Wilson, *The Theory of Island Biogeography* (Princeton, N.J.: Princeton University Press, 1967).

98. E.R. Pianka, "On r-and K-selection," *American Naturalist* 104 (1970): 592–97. The terms r and K refer, respectively, to the intrinsic rate of natural increase and the carrying capacity, as they appear in the equation for the "S"-shaped population growth curve.

99. Odum, *Fundamentals of Ecology;* Garrett Hardin, "The Cybernetics of Competition: A Biologist's View of Society," *Perspectives in Biology and Medicine* 7 (1963): 58–84.

100. C.S. Holling, "The Components of Predation as Revealed by a Study of Small-Mammal Predation of the European Pine Sawfly," *Canadian Entomologist* 91 (1959): 293–320.

101. John Vandermeer, "The Interference Production Principle: An Ecological Theory for Agriculture," *BioScience* 31 (1981): 361–64.

102. J.A. Browning, "Relevance of Knowledge About Natural Ecosystems to Development of Pest Management Programs for Agro-Ecosystems," *Proceedings of the American Phytopathological Society* 1 (1975): 191–99.

103. Clark et al., "On the Scope and Value of Ecology."

104. W.C. Clarke, "Progressing with the Past: Environmentally Sustainable Modifications to Traditional Agricultural Systems," in E.K. Fisk, ed., *The Adaptation of Traditional Agriculture: Socioeconomic Problems of Urbanization* (Australian National University Develop-

ment Studies Centre Monograph No. 11, 1978), pp. 142–57; T. Allen Lambert, ''Energy and Entropy in American Agriculture and Rural Society: A New Paradigm for Public Policy Analysis,'' *Cornell Journal of Social Relations* 15 (1980): 84–97.

105. Conway, ''What is an Agroecosystem and Why is it Worthy of Study?''

106. Lowrance et al., *Agricultural Ecosystems;* for an example of a national-level use of the term, see Vaclav Smil, ''China's Agro-Ecosystem,'' *Agro-Ecosystems* 7 (1981): 27–46.

107. C.A. Francis, C.A. Flor, and S.R. Temple, ''Adapting Varieties for Intercropping Systems in the Tropics,'' in R.I. Papendick, P.A. Sanchez, and G.B. Triplett, eds., *Multiple Cropping* (Madison, Wisc.: American Society of Agronomy, ASA Special Publication No. 27, 1976), pp. 235–53.

108. Otto Soemarwoto et al., ''The Javanese Home-Garden as an Integrated Agro-Ecosystem,'' in *Science for a Better Environment: Proceedings of International Congress of Scientists on the Human Environment (HESC)*, Kyoto, Japan, November 1975; Widagda, ''An Ecosystem Analysis of West-Javanese Home Gardens.''

109. Widagda, ''An Ecosystem Analysis of West-Javanese Home Gardens.''

110. Matthias U. Igbozurike, ''Ecological Balance in Tropical Agriculture,'' *Geographical Review* 61 (1971): 519–29.

111. *Ibid.*

112. B.R. Trenbath, ''Biomass Productivity of Mixtures,'' *Advances in Agronomy* 26 (1974): 177–210.

113. Stephen R. Gliessman, ''Multiple Cropping Systems: A Basis for Developing an Alternative Agriculture,'' in OTA, *Innovative Biological Technologies for Lesser Developed Countries—Workshop Proceedings*, pp. 69–83.

114. Trenbath, ''Biomass Productivity of Mixtures.''

115. Sanchez, *Properties and Management of Soils in the Tropics.*

116. S.R. Gliessman and A.M. Amador, ''Ecological Aspects of Production in Traditional Agroecosystems in the Humid Lowland Tropics of Mexico,'' *Tropical Ecology and Development* (1980): 601–608; Gliessman, ''Multiple Cropping Systems: A Basis for Developing an Alternative Agriculture.''

117. H.J.W. Mutsaers, "Mixed Cropping Experiments with Maize and Groundnuts," *Netherlands Journal of Agricultural Science* 26 (1978): 344–53.

118. Jerry L. McIntosh, Suryatna Effendi, and Inu Gandana Ismail, "Productivity of Tropical Upland Soils Can be Maintained and Improved," *Indonesian Agricultural Research and Development Journal* 2 (1980): 13–16.

119. Long Yiming and Zhang Jiahe, "Ecological Effects and Economic Results of the Artificial Plant Community," presented at the Workshop on Ecosystem Models for Development, Kunming and Guangzhou, China, Sept. 27–Oct. 9, 1982.

120. Donald R. Sumner, Ben Doupnik, Jr., and M.G. Boosalis, "Effects of Reduced Tillage and Multiple Cropping on Plant Diseases," *Annual Review of Phytopathology* 19 (1981): 167–87.

121. Miguel A. Altieri, Deborah K. Letourneau, and James R. Davis, "The Requirements of Sustainable Agroecosystems," in Douglass, *Agricultural Sustainability in a Changing World Order*, pp. 175–89.

122. R.M. Perrin, "Pest Management in Multiple Cropping Systems," *Agro-Ecosystems* 3 (1977): 93–118.

123. J.C. Tahvanainen and R.B. Root, "The Influence of Vegetational Diversity on the Population of a Specialized Herbivore *Phyllotreta cruciferae*," *Oecologia* 10 (1972): 321–46.

124. Perrin, "Pest Management in Multiple Cropping Systems."

125. *Ibid.*

126. Stephen J. Risch, David Andow, and Miguel A. Altieri, "Agroecosystem Diversity and Pest Control: Data, Tentative Conclusions, and New Research Directions," *Environmental Entomology* 12 (1983): 625–29.

127. David Andow, "Effect of Agricultural Diversity on Insect Populations," in Wiiliam Lockeretz, ed., *Environmentally Sound Agriculture* (New York, Praeger, 1983), pp. 91–115.

128. Altieri et al., "The Requirements of Sustainable Agroecosystems."

129. Alan R. Putnam and William B. Duke, "Allelopathy in Agroecosystems," *Annual Review of Phytopathology* 16 (1978): 431–51; M.A. Altieri and J.D. Doll, "The Potential of Allelopathy as a

Tool for Weed Management in Crop Fields," *PANS* 24 (1978): 495–502.

130. J.C. Chacon and S.R. Gliessman, "Use of the 'Non-Weed' Concept in Traditional Tropical Agroecosystems of South-Eastern Mexico," *Agro-Ecosystems* 8 (1982): 1–11.

131. S.C. Datta and A.K. Banerjee, "Useful Weeds of West Bengal Rice Fields," *Economic Botany* 32 (1978): 297–310.

132. Igbozurike, "Ecological Balance in Tropical Agriculture."

133. Gliessman, "Multiple Cropping Systems"; Altieri, *Agroecology*. Although developing countries commonly have labor surpluses, the labor needs in agriculture are often sporadic, especially in monocultures. Polyculture systems that involve planting, harvesting, and other labor-intensive activities throughout the growing season are more likely to make full use of the rural labor force.

134. Trenbath, "Biomass Productivity of Mixtures"; Gliessman, "Multiple Cropping Systems"; Altieri, *Agroecology*; Perrin, "Pest Management in Multiple Cropping Systems"; D.J. Andrews and A.H. Kassam, "The Importance of Multiple Cropping in Increasing World Food Supplies," in R.I. Papendick et al., *Multiple Cropping*, pp. 1–10.

135. Andrews and Kassam, "The Importance of Multiple Cropping in Increasing World Food Supplies"; Francis et al., "Adapting Varieties for Intercropping Systems in the Tropics."

136. This section is based on S.R. Gliessman, R. Garcia, and M. Amador, "The Ecological Basis for the Application of Traditional Agricultural Technology in the Management of Tropical Agro-Ecosystems," *Agro-Ecosystems* 7 (1981): 173–85, and related references.

137. Arturo Gomez-Pompa, "An Old Answer to the Future," *Mazingira* 5 (1978): 50–55.

138. Otto Soemarwoto, "Nitrogen in Tropical Agriculture: Indonesia as a Case Study," *Ambio* 6 (1977): 162–65.

139. Dr. Anthony Bellotti, International Center for Tropical Agriculture, private communication.

140. Widagda, "An Ecosystem Analysis of West-Javanese Home Gardens."

141. James Sholto Douglas and Robert A. de J. Hart, *Forest Farming: Towards a Solution to Problems of World Hunger and Conservation* (London: Robinson and Watkins, 1976); Gonzalo De Las Salas, ed., *Proceedings of Workshop on Agro-Forestry Systems in Latin America* (Turrialba, Costa Rica: Centro Agronomico de Investigación y Enseñanza, 1979); L.H. MacDonald, ed., *Agro-Forestry in the African Humid Tropics* (Tokyo: United Nations University, 1981).

142. Wilson and Kang, ''Developing Stable and Productive Biological Cropping Systems for the Humid Tropics.''

143. Napoleon T. Vergara, ''Integral Agro-Forestry: A Potential Strategy for Stabilizing Shifting Cultivation and Sustaining Productivity of the Natural Environment,'' Environment and Policy Institute, East-West Center Working Paper, May 1981.

144. *Ibid.*

145. J. Combe and G. Budowski, ''Classification of Agro-Forestry Techniques,'' in De Las Salas, *Proceedings of Workshop on Agro-Forestry Systems in Latin America*, pp. 17–47.

146. Vergara, ''Integral Agro-Forestry.''

147. Napoleon T. Vergara, ed., *New Directions in Agroforestry: The Potential of Tropical Legume Trees* (Honolulu, Hawaii: Environment and Policy Institute, East-West Center, 1982).

148. Wilson and Kang, ''Developing Stable and Productive Biological Cropping Systems for the Humid Tropics.''

149. Michael McGuahey, ''Impact of Forestry Initiatives in the Sahel'' (Washington, D.C.: Chemonics International, 1986).

150. *Ibid.*

151. Steve Dennison, ''The Majjia Valley Windbreak Evaluation Study: An Examination of Progress and Analyses to Date,'' unpublished report for CARE, February 1986.

152. Friedrich Behmel and Irmfried Neumann, ''An Example of Agro-Forestry in Tropical Mountain Areas,'' in L.H. MacDonald, *Agro-Forestry in the African Humid Tropics*, pp. 92–98.

153. Sajise, ''Grassland Regeneration Strategy for Small Upland Farmers.''

154. J. Lazier, A. Getahun, and M. Velez, "The Integration of Livestock Production in Agro-Forestry," in L.H. MacDonald, *Agro-Forestry in the African Humid Tropics*, pp. 84–88.

155. John P. Bishop, "Tropical Forest Sheep on Legume Forage/Fuelwood Fallows," *Agroforestry Systems* 1 (1983): 79–84.

156. J.P. Andriesse, "From Shifting Agriculture to Agroforestry or Permanent Agriculture?", *Proceedings of the 50th Symposium on Tropical Agriculture* (Amsterdam: Royal Tropical Institute, 1979), Bulletin 303, pp. 35–43.

157. McGuahey, "Impact of Forestry Initiatives in the Sahel."

158. Charito Medina, "Evaluation of Ipil-ipil *(Leucaena leucocephala)* and Kakwate (*Gliricidia sepium*) as Biological Contour Strips for Productive and Protective Upland Farming," presented at Symposium on Research on Impact of Development on Human Activity Systems in Southeast Asia, Bandung, Indonesia, August 1983.

159. Conway, "Agroecosystem Analysis"; Conway, "What is an Agroecosystem and Why is it Worthy of Study?"

160. A. Terry Rambo, "Human Ecology Research on Rural Development," in A. Terry Rambo, John A. Dixon, and Wu Tsechin, eds., *Ecosystem Models for Development* (Honolulu, Hawaii, Environment and Policy Institute, East-West Center, Honolulu, Hawaii, 1984), pp. 6–27; A. Terry Rambo, "Applied Human Ecology Research on Asian Agricultural Systems," presented at Workshop on Human Ecology Research on Agroecosystems, Nanjing, China, September 1985.

161. Sajise, "Regeneration of Critical Upland Areas: An Ecological Imperative."

162. Rambo, "Human Ecology Research on Rural Development"; Rambo, "Applied Human Ecology Research on Asian Agricultural Systems."

163. Behmel and Neumann, "An Example of Agro-Forestry in Tropical Mountain Areas."

164. M. Peter McPherson, remarks to Workshop on Regenerative Farming Systems, Washington, D.C., December 1985.

165. Irmfried Neumann, lecture presented at the World Bank, September 1982.

166. Worldwatch Institute, *The State of the World* (New York: Norton, 1986).

167. Dover, *A Better Mousetrap.*

168. Edens and Koenig, ''Agroecosystem Management in a Resource-Limited World''; Thomas C. Edens and Dean L. Haynes, ''Closed System Agriculture: Resource Constraints, Management Options, and Design Alternatives,'' *Annual Review of Phytopathology* 20 (1982): 363–95.

169. Christopher J.N. Gibbs, ''Agricultural Systems Research in Asia: A Comparative Discussion of Human Ecology, Agroecosystems Research, Farming Systems Research, and Cropping Systems Research,'' presented to Second SUAN Symposium, Baguio, Philippines, March 1985.

170. Conway, ''Agroecosystem Analysis.''

171. Gibbs, ''Agricultural Systems Research in Asia.''

172. Office of Technology Assessment, *Innovative Biological Technologies for Lesser Developed Countries—Workshop Proceedings.*

173. Robert Repetto, *Paying the Price: Pesticide Subsidies in Developing Countries* (Washington, D.C.: World Resources Institute, 1985).

174. Sajise, ''Upland Community Development: Some Ecological Considerations.''

175. *Ibid.*

176. R.W. Cummings and J.S. Robins, ''Setting Priorities in Food and Agricultural Research,'' *Horizon* (October 1983): 28–33.

177. Office of Technology Assessment, *Innovative Biological Technologies for Lesser Developed Countries—Workshop Proceedings.*

178. Remarks of various AID officials at the Workshop on Regenerative Farming Systems, Washington, D.C., December 1985.

179. Nancy Shute, ''After a Turbulent Youth, the Peace Corps Grows Up,'' *Smithsonian* 16 (February 1986): 80–89.

180. James O. Morgan, ''Programmatic Implementation of Regenerative Agriculture,'' presented at Workshop on Regenerative Farming Systems, Washington, D.C., December 1985.

181. Edens and Koenig, "Agroecosystem Management in a Resource-Limited World"; Edens and Haynes, "Closed System Agriculture." *Annual Review of Phytopathology* 20 (1982): 363-95.

182. Charles A. Francis, "Agricultural Policy," presented at Workshop on Regenerative Farming Systems, Washington, D.C., December 1985; Abregana et al., "Comprehensive Small-Scale Upland Agroforestry"; Miguel A. Altieri, "Developing Pest Management Strategies for Small Farmers Based on Traditional Knowledge," *Bulletin of the Institute for Development Anthropology* 3 (1985): 13-18; Altieri, *Agroecology*.

183. Gliessman, "Multiple Cropping Systems: A Basis for Developing an Alternative Agriculture."

184. W.C. Liebhardt, C.A. Francis, and M. Sands, "Research Needs for the Development of Resource Efficient Technologies," presented at Workshop on Regenerative Farming Systems, Washington, D.C., December 1985.

185. Dover, *A Better Mousetrap*.

186. Altieri, *Agroecology*.

187. Repetto, *Paying the Price*.

188. Miguel A. Altieri, "The Question of Small Farm Development: Who Teaches Whom?" *Agriculture, Ecosystems, and Environment* 9 (1983): 401-5.

189. Joshua Mukusya, "The Utooni Experience," presented at Workshop on Regenerative Farming Systems, Washington, D.C., December 1985.

WRI PUBLICATIONS ORDER FORM

ORDER NO.	TITLE	QTY	TOTAL $
S789	*To Feed The Earth: Agroecology for Sustainable Development* by Michael J. Dover and Lee M. Talbot, 1987, $10.00		
S710	*A Matter of Degrees: The Potential for Controlling the Greenhouse Effect* by Irving M. Mintzer, 1987, $10.00		
S792	*Skimming the Water: Rent-Seeking and the Performance of Public Irrigation Systems* by Robert Repetto, 1986, $10.00		
S783	*The Sky is the Limit: Strategies for Protecting the Ozone Layer* by Alan S. Miller and Irving M. Mintzer, 1986, $10.00		
S781	*Double Dividends? U.S. Biotechnology and Third World Development* by John Elkington, 1986, $10.00		
B719	*Bordering on Trouble: Resources and Politics in Latin America* edited by Andrew Maguire and Janet Welsh Brown, 1986, $14.95 (paperback)		
S784	*Troubled Waters: New Policies for Managing Water in the American West* by Mohamed T. El-Ashry and Diana C. Gibbons, 1986, $10.00.		
S712	*Growing Power: Bioenergy for Development and Industry* by Alan S. Miller, Irving M. Mintzer, and Sara H. Hoagland, 1986, $10.00.		
S725	*Down to Business: Multinational Corporations, the Environment, and Development* by Charles S. Pearson, 1985, $10.00		
B723	*The Global Possible: Resources, Development, and the New Century* edited by Robert Repetto, 1986, $13.95 (paperback); $45.00 (cloth)		
B732	*World Enough and Time: Successful Strategies for Resource Management* by Robert Repetto, 1986, $5.95 (paperback); $16.00 (cloth)		
S724	*Getting Tough: Public Policy and the Management of Pesticide Resistance* by Michael Dover and Brian Croft, 1984, $10.00		
S714	*Field Duty: U.S. Farmworkers and Pesticide Safety* by Robert F. Wasserstrom and Richard Wiles, 1985, $10.00		
S716	*A Better Mousetrap: Improving Pest Management for Agriculture* by Michael J. Dover, 1985, $10.00		
S717	*The American West's Acid Rain Test* by Philip Roth, Charles Blanchard, John Harte, Harvey Michaels, and Mohamed El-Ashry, 1985, $10.00		
S715	*Paying the Price: Pesticide Subsidies in Developing Countries* by Robert Repetto, 1985, $10.00		
S776	*The World Bank and Agricultural Development: An Insider's View* by Montague Yudelman, 1985, $10.00		
S731	*Tropical Forests: A Call for Action*, 1985 by WRI, The World Bank and UNDP, $12.50		
S726	*Helping Developing Countries Help Themselves: Toward a Congressional Agenda for Improved Resource and Environmental Management in the Third World* (a WRI working paper) by Lee M. Talbot, 1985, $10.00		
B780	*World Resources 1987*, $16.95 (paperback); $32.95 (cloth)		
	WRI SUBSCRIPTION $50. ($70 for overseas)		
	SUBTOTAL		
	Postage and Handling		$2.00
	TOTAL DUE		

BECOME A WRI SUBSCRIBER

■ Receive all WRI Policy Studies, all WRI research reports, and occasional publications for calendar year 1987—including *World Resources 1987*. If you join in March, for example, you will immediately receive publications issued in January and February. $50.00. ($70.00 outside of the United States.)

■ Discounts available for bulk orders.

Name   (last)   (first)

Place of Work

Street Address

City/State   Postal Code/Country

Please send check or money order (U.S. dollars only) to WRI Publications, P.O. Box 620, Holmes, PA 19043-0620, U.S.A.

WRI PUBLICATIONS ORDER FORM

ORDER NO.	TITLE	QTY	TOTAL $
S789	*To Feed The Earth: Agroecology for Sustainable Development* by Michael J. Dover and Lee M. Talbot, 1987, $10.00		
S710	*A Matter of Degrees: The Potential for Controlling the Greenhouse Effect* by Irving M. Mintzer, 1987, $10.00		
S792	*Skimming the Water: Rent-Seeking and the Performance of Public Irrigation Systems* by Robert Repetto, 1986, $10.00		
S783	*The Sky is the Limit: Strategies for Protecting the Ozone Layer* by Alan S. Miller and Irving M. Mintzer, 1986, $10.00		
S781	*Double Dividends? U.S. Biotechnology and Third World Development* by John Elkington, 1986, $10.00		
B719	*Bordering on Trouble: Resources and Politics in Latin America* edited by Andrew Maguire and Janet Welsh Brown, 1986, $14.95 (paperback)		
S784	*Troubled Waters: New Policies for Managing Water in the American West* by Mohamed T. El-Ashry and Diana C. Gibbons, 1986, $10.00.		
S712	*Growing Power: Bioenergy for Development and Industry* by Alan S. Miller, Irving M. Mintzer, and Sara H. Hoagland, 1986, $10.00.		
S725	*Down to Business: Multinational Corporations, the Environment, and Development* by Charles S. Pearson, 1985, $10.00		
B723	*The Global Possible: Resources, Development, and the New Century* edited by Robert Repetto, 1986, $13.95 (paperback); $45.00 (cloth)		
B732	*World Enough and Time: Successful Strategies for Resource Management* by Robert Repetto, 1986, $5.95 (paperback); $16.00 (cloth)		
S724	*Getting Tough: Public Policy and the Management of Pesticide Resistance* by Michael Dover and Brian Croft, 1984, $10.00		
S714	*Field Duty: U.S. Farmworkers and Pesticide Safety* by Robert F. Wasserstrom and Richard Wiles, 1985, $10.00		
S716	*A Better Mousetrap: Improving Pest Management for Agriculture* by Michael J. Dover, 1985, $10.00		
S717	*The American West's Acid Rain Test* by Philip Roth, Charles Blanchard, John Harte, Harvey Michaels, and Mohamed El-Ashry, 1985, $10.00		
S715	*Paying the Price: Pesticide Subsidies in Developing Countries* by Robert Repetto, 1985, $10.00		
S776	*The World Bank and Agricultural Development: An Insider's View* by Montague Yudelman, 1985, $10.00		
S731	*Tropical Forests: A Call for Action*, 1985 by WRI, The World Bank and UNDP, $12.50		
S726	*Helping Developing Countries Help Themselves: Toward a Congressional Agenda for Improved Resource and Environmental Management in the Third World* (a WRI working paper) by Lee M. Talbot, 1985, $10.00		
B780	*World Resources 1987*, $16.95 (paperback); $32.95 (cloth)		
	WRI SUBSCRIPTION $50. ($70 for overseas)		
	SUBTOTAL		
	Postage and Handling		$2.00
	TOTAL DUE		

BECOME A WRI SUBSCRIBER

■ Receive all WRI Policy Studies, all WRI research reports, and occasional publications for calendar year 1987—including *World Resources 1987*. If you join in March, for example, you will immediately receive publications issued in January and February. $50.00. ($70.00 outside of the United States.)

■ Discounts available for bulk orders.

Name   (last)   (first)

Place of Work

Street Address

City/State   Postal Code/Country

Please send check or money order (U.S. dollars only) to WRI Publications, P.O. Box 620, Holmes, PA 19043-0620, U.S.A.